Western Regio
non-passenger trains

Compiled by Jeremy Clements

The
· Transport ·
Treasury

On 3rd September 1955, Class 28xx No 2824 was leading an Up Class F unfitted express freight past Old Oak Common with a rake of at least 45 closed vans. This locomotive was built in January 1907, and went through the whole gamut of developments applied to Britain's first 2-8-0 class:- a series of boiler improvements; application of superheating in March 1910; installation of outside steam pipes and curved front drop end in July 1946. Withdrawal came in August 1959 at the conclusion of a long and honourable career undertaking the sort of duties illustrated here. *RCR Ref 6101-7100 (396).*

© Images and design: The Transport Treasury 2020. Text Jeremy Clements

ISBN 978-1-913251-08-6

First Published in 2020 by Transport Treasury Publishing Ltd. 16 Highworth Close, High Wycombe, HP13 7PJ

www.ttpublishing.co.uk

Printed in the UK by Henry Ling Limited, at the Dorset Press, Dorchester. DT1 1HD.

Contents

Front cover: Castle Class No 5034 *Corfe Castle* was carrying *The Torbay Express* headboard as it led 11 or 12 vans off the Torbay branch on 18th July 1958. This engine had earlier worked the Down express through to Kingswear and after turning, the most convenient means of moving it back to Newton Abbot was by this revenue-earning service so avoiding the use of a scarce path on this congested route. Despite the incongruity, the headboard and the train reporting number (officially the 12.00 am Paddington-Kingswear – Down Torbay Express) were probably best left in situ. The headcode defines the train as a Class J Mineral or empty wagon train.

Evidence of a busy network is found in the three corridor coaches stowed in the short siding beside the Down Torbay line, on which route siding space was at a premium during high summer. The foreshortening of the image makes it hard to determine the exact position of the water column in the V of Aller Junction. It seems to have been placed for the convenience of engines waiting for the road before coming off the Torbay line. Curiously the column stands this side of the junction approach signal presumably for sighting purposes so it could be only accessed with the board "off". *RCR Ref 11801-12900 (686).*

Title page: In an era when branch lines formed an integral part of the distributive network for goods by rail, small prairie No 4561 is arriving at Brent with the 7.30 pm from Kingsbridge on 8th June 1961. This combination had been photographed earlier leaving Brent as the 6.45 pm. The train comprises an ex-SR 4-wheel utility van for delivery and collection of parcels and small goods, and a Hawksworth era, BR-built, non-corridor Brake Composite of Diagram E167 (the number from another view indicates that it might be No W6279W). Built in 1954, these spacious coaches enjoyed short careers as all had succumbed to the DMU invasion by 1963. *PG Ref 2560.*

Introduction

The Great Western Railway was primarily a freight transporter, from the 1840s onward consistently generating more gross revenue from goods traffic than it ever did from the conveyance of people. This pattern was sustained following the company's enlargement through the Grouping, as evidenced by annual gross receipts:

£ millions	1923	1932	1937
Freight	18.3	13.8	16.4
Passenger	10.6	7.6	8.5

Source: The Railway Research Service Survey - 1st June 1938.

Freight income was thus crucial to the company's fortunes and it is significant that in 1937, not long before the system suffered the depredations of wartime conditions, it accounted for almost double the earnings from passenger services. Perhaps not immediately obvious but nonetheless significant was that the freight earnings were more robust and thus financially speaking of better quality under adverse conditions. The worst trading year (1932) saw freight income decline proportionately less during that period than did passenger receipts. This resilience essentially derived from the diverse range of cargoes handled. The views in this work are a distillation of trains that moved coal and other minerals, raw materials, scrap metal, manufactured components, motor vehicles, completed items of machinery, agricultural and dairy produce, livestock, fruit and vegetables, flowers, personal effects and parcels.

Many services ran during the night hours and so escaped photographers' cameras. Newspaper trains and the majority of mail services operated entirely in darkness while of the accelerated freight services, approximately 60% had scheduled departure times between 7.00 pm and midnight while 25% started their journeys during the small hours. Despite working in daylight, less prestigious services might be overlooked on account of their lacking the glamour of express passenger trains and in their use of more humble motive power. However, diversity was as evident at the front end as in the loads hauled; in this work every GWR 4-6-0 class from the Saints onward makes an appearance. Bearing in mind that more mundane duties often attracted older machines, non-passenger trains thus accounted for a broader spectrum of locomotive types.

The Great Western's goods business survived the war virtually intact, not only in its operating pattern but also in the physical and organisational infrastructure. The writings of the late Tony Atkins comprehensively surveyed operating methods including the developed science of optimised train assembly, and the processes applied to minimise non-revenue earning light engine and shunting movements. Tony's studies of the company's cartage activities illustrate the effectiveness of inter-modal functions in serving the many locations that the railway could not physically reach. A significant spin-off was the movement of loads that did not involve trains at all – a prescient indicator of the ascendancy of road over rail for so much of the nation's inland trade. Holistically, the GWR's goods business (and hence that of BR Western Region) was an undertaking of astonishing complexity that worked with greater efficiency than is generally acknowledged.

--- o O o ---

This album relies on the work of two accomplished photographers who shared an enthusiasm for the Great Western Railway and its nationalised successor, but who came to prominence through quite different means.

Dick Riley lived in south London and the Southern represented the largest element of his vast portfolio. However, his fascination with the GWR dated from the late 1930s and his pre-war work, mainly of static subjects, has a particular importance in often portraying ageing locomotive types in the winter of their careers. After wartime military service, his post-war professional career in the City largely confined his camera work to evenings, Saturday afternoons and Sundays. Fortunately for Swindon devotees, several annual holidays were spent in the West Country. The volume of images produced during those fortnights certainly prompts the question how much time he actually spent with his family. Nevertheless, those who can recall with great

Mainline freight

On 18th April 1956, Class 43xx No 5318 was heading a Down train of Tippler wagons loaded with ironstone through Harbury Cutting between Southam Road & Harbury and Leamington Spa. This locomotive had worked in slightly heavier form as No 8318 from 1926 until 1944 when it reverted to its original condition as seen here. It survived in service until September 1961 without ever receiving the outside steam pipes fitted to so many of the class. *RCR Ref 6101-7100 (838).*

nostalgia those magical steam-filled summers gratefully acknowledge his personal devotion, and his family's patience and forbearance.

He considered that his abilities only matured fully from 1954 onwards, in connection with the start of his association with the great Maurice Earley. Recognition of his work meant that several authors approached him for images to include in their publications, and his generosity resulted in their broad distribution throughout railway literature. The appearance of his artistry in so many different works has complicated attempts to limit images to those previously unpublished.

Peter Gray's images were also widely distributed but in an unusual manner. A long-time resident of Torquay with the GWR on his doorstep, he assiduously recorded operations close to home, using several favoured locations, mainly in Devon, while also paying attention to the other means of rail travel in the region. In 1984, an approach to the Editor of Torquay's *Herald Express* newspaper led to a regular Saturday feature under the series title "Rail Trail". Each week, a photograph from his collection (mainly his own work) appeared together with an extended caption that described the technical aspects of the locomotive and train portrayed, and also the broader context of its presence within the local railway scene.

This newspaper series might have been considered an indulgence towards an ageing minority of train spotters in recalling events more than a quarter of a century earlier. However, interest was excited among a readership that might otherwise not have volunteered a particular leaning towards trains. Perhaps there were more closet rail fans than had been hitherto recognised or perhaps cherished recollections of a simpler, sunnier past had been nostalgically reawakened.

Whatever the reasons, anticipating the GW150 celebrations of 1985, the series was sustained by its continuing popularity over the following seven years and more. Cuttings of the articles were distributed well beyond Torbay, regularly reaching New Zealand in one case. Ninety-two of the articles appeared in *Rail Trails: South West* (Silver Link Publishing Ltd 1992).

Unfortunately, most railway goods services, for all their organisational effectiveness could not match the journey speeds, flexibility, and door-to-door convenience of that is possible with modern road transport using a tailor-made motorway network. The operating demands imposed by the "just-in-time" regimes of modern trade and commerce changed customer preferences and saw termination of this varied aspect of the railway world.

Jeremy Clements, Co Meath 2020.

Chapter 1
Mainline freight

In December 1954, British Railways published its Modernisation Plan which was intended to eliminate deficits through improvements in route capacity, operating reliability and service speeds. These laudable objectives were focussed on redressing the results of intensive use and maintenance deficiencies from the war years, and of underinvestment in the following period. A major objective was construction of new marshalling yards and an up-grade of existing facilities to accelerate the handling of single wagon loads, then an important part of BR's vast freight business, as inherited from the Big Four.

Unfortunately, the Plan was an inwardly focussed document that assessed the need for overdue improvement in the railway's infrastructure while failing to recognise the changing pattern of the freight market at large. World War 2 had stimulated the urgent development of techniques to move large volumes of equipment and

materials speedily and efficiently. The humble pallet and the fork lift truck had revolutionised the time required to load and unload a motor lorry, a vehicle that has innate operating flexibility and door-to-door delivery capacity. By contrast, the vast majority of rail freight is subject to intermodal constraints at start and finish of each journey, unless both supplier and consumer enjoy on-site rail access.

A further disadvantage for freight by rail was operating speed. Progress had been made with vacuum-braked express services, effectively the precursor of the modern block train that moves homogeneous bulk cargos with elapsed journey timings comparable with many passenger services. However, much of the freight vehicle fleet remained primitive in design, inadequately braked, with sub-optimal load capacities while requiring periodic physical inspection *en route* over any significant distance. Progressive

The crowded railway. This scene near Par on 30th August 1954 illustrates the intensity of summer operations in the 1950s. Churchward mogul No 6397 on a Class A mixed freight has been side-lined in a loop to allow the passage of an Ordinary or Stopping Down passenger train hauled by No 6817 *Gwenddwr Grange*. At the same time, an Up goods train curves away into the distance with the guard surveying the scene from the trailing balcony of his Toad. *RCR Ref 5100-6100 (337).*

elements within the sector's senior management had recognised the cost and inconvenience of hopelessly out-dated operating methods even before World War 1. Improvements were achieved during that conflict through creation of the pool system for railway company-owned wagons but efforts to rationalise the incubus of the private owner system were stymied by vested interests and short-sightedness. By 1948, the bleak fact remained that while improvements had been made in buffers, drawgear and manual brakes, the typical British wagon had changed little over the preceding 100 years. It reflected few, if any, of the technological advances that typified its counterpart in America, continental Europe and even the railway systems of the then British Empire.

Interest rates played a crucial factor in the demise of traditional rail freight. Even in the 1940s and 1950s, there was growing awareness of the importance of minimised transit times. A load that had to be moved from supplier to railhead, loaded into a wagon, collected for transit to marshalling yard, assembled with others into a full train, then moved at little more than pedestrian pace to its destination for the whole process to be reversed, represented unusable inventory which someone had to finance. The motorway programme and general up-grade of the road system, for all the concomitant disadvantages of pollution and occasional delaying congestion, yielded savings in time and financial cost that the traditional rail network could never match.

Modern container systems, block trains, and unified loads form an essential, highly efficient part of the modern railway system but here are some reminders of the diversity and individuality that the made mainline freight of past years so fascinating.

Class 43xx No 5317 was approaching Laira, Plymouth on 3rd September 1954 with a Class F unfitted freight comprising around 14 wagons, mainly closed vans. The train has been switched to the North Quay branch and has almost completed the crossing from the Down main. The brake van which seems to be a BR type rather than an ex-GWR Toad is just passing in front of a pannier tank which is held on the headshunt at signals protecting the junction. *RCR Ref 5001-6100 (409).*

Opposite top: The large prairies were genuine mixed traffic machines, equally at home on suburban and medium distance passenger services, as pilots or bankers on assisting duties, and on substantial freight trains over quite long distances. On 22nd October 1954, Class 5101 No 5170 passes Aynho station southwards towards Oxford on a lengthy Class B through freight. In the right background can be seen the embankment of the Paddington-Birmingham Down line that crosses the Didcot-Birmingham route by means of a flying junction, which in this view is hidden by the station goods shed. *RCR Ref 5001-6100 (581)*.

Opposite bottom: On the move again. In this immediate sequel to the previous view on 22nd October 1954, No 6963 *Throwley Hall*, which has been standing in the loop to the south of Aynho, has just been given the road. It is drawing out on to the main line at the head of another Class B freight to continue its journey towards Birmingham, just as No 5170 passes. *RCR Ref 5001-6100 (583)*.

This page: No 5962 *Wantage Hall* approaching Birmingham Snow Hill on 21st March 1960 with a train composed of well over 20 apparently empty wagons running under the head code for a Class D stopping goods. Most of the wagons in view are more modern steel-bodied vehicles but the 6th, 10th and 13th are older timber-bodied vehicles whose presence by then was being whittled away. *RCR Ref 14000-15099 (576)*.

Mainline freight

Opposite top: page: A characteristic feature of a mainline passenger journey was the succession of goods trains side-lined awaiting a clear road, as in this view of Castle Class No 5062 *Earl of Shaftesbury* overtaking 2-8-0 Class 2884 No 3843 which was standing in the Down loop at Tilehurst on Saturday, 1st August 1959. A small mystery relates to the Train Reporting Number 215 chalked on the smokebox door as that summer, this related solely to the Weekdays Only 5.00 pm Paddington – Weston-super-Mare. Dick Riley recorded this train as a Saturdays Only Paddington-Bristol service which does not appear in the official lists. *RCR Refs 14000-15099 (23).*

Opposite bottom: With Castle No 5062 and its train now out of section, No 3843 is re-joining the Down main at Tilehurst on 1st August 1959. According to the head code, the grimy 2-8-0 is hauling a Class A goods but this seems doubtful as much of the train apparently consists of timber-bodied open wagons of varying vintages. Little can be discerned of their identities but the third is a 7-plank open with a P-prefix number whichy confirms its private owner provenance. That this is a Dick Riley photograph is confirmed by his faithful Morris Minor Tourer parked to the extreme right. *RCR Refs 14000-15099 (26).*

Below: The Granges seemed to turn up with almost any category of train except the fastest passenger services. No 6826 *Nannerth Grange* was entering Plymouth North Road station on 8th April 1960 with what is recorded as a ballast train although the load looks more like concrete sleepers. The Class D head code defines a ballast train with not less than one-third of the vehicles piped to the engine. *RCR Ref 14000-15099 (611).*

Opposite: Class 2884 No 3821 of Stourbridge shed passes Worcester shed on 15th April 1956 with a Class H through freight working. Although the standard steel-bodied 16-ton mineral wagon was rapidly penetrating BR's fleet, older ex-private owner timber-bodied vehicles remained much in evidence as here.

Also, to the left of the locomotive, a BR mineral wagon is sandwiched between two ex-PO wagons, readily identified by their running numbers. That to the left shows evidence of its original livery (apparently "Stanton") but now bearing the number P129474. This was allocated in the exercise initiated by British Railways in 1949 to apply the P-prefixed number series to the huge, heterogeneous fleet requisitioned by the government in September 1939. The introduction of new all-steel mineral wagons outpaced this renumbering programme which was abandoned in 1957 before its completion. No P129474 was one that was contracted to be maintained by Wagon Repairs Ltd. *RCR Ref 5001-6100 (749)*.

Above: Pannier tanks the Class 57xx/ 8750 were doughty performers but No 3659 gives the impression that it might be punching above its weight with this pick-up goods on 14th July 1955. The train consists of at least 30 wagons and most likely has come off the Torbay branch, bound for Hackney Yard immediately to the east of Newton Abbot. On the climb from Torquay, rear end assistance was probably needed. *RCR Ref 5001-6100 (835)*.

Above: Churchward's 2-6-0 Class 43xx was a late addition to his seminal Locomotive Scheme of January 1901, not appearing until over ten years later. The Mogul concept owed much to contemporary practice in the United States and this type became the most numerous design introduced under his tenure. Its "maid of all work" role led to postponement of the 5' 8" driving wheel 4-6-0 proposal until 1936 when the Granges first appeared. No 6388 was one 35 moguls supplied in 1921-2 by Robert Stephenson & Co, the first new locomotives to be built for the GWR by a commercial manufacturer in many years.

Working wrong line, No 6388 was approaching Evesham from the Worcester direction on 29th April 1956 with a train of ballast wagons, apparently loaded with spoil. The 29th was a Sunday and the presence of a Toad at either end indicates that the mogul has departed from a section subject to permanent way works and line occupation. The headcode is unclear being that for a light engine with up to two brake vans; an additional lamp on the smokebox door indicating a Class H ballast train would seem more appropriate. *RCR Ref 5001-6100 (890).*

Opposite top: Journey times for pick-up goods trains could be significantly extended by the requirement to attach/ detach wagons at intermediate stations. This would seem to the lot of 0-6-0 Class 2251 No 2222 at Banbury on 30th April 1956; its headcode denoted a Class J pick-up or branch goods. *RCR Ref 5001-6100 (907).*

Opposite bottom: 2-8-2T Class 72xx No 7200 was descending Stoneycombe Gorge on 22nd August 1949. Originally, this locomotive was the first of a 20-strong batch of 2-8-0T Class 42xx (numbered 5275 to 5294) built between July and October 1930. Intended to handle heavy South Wales coal traffic, the timing was unfortunate as that industry was then in serious decline and the need for these powerful machines was contracting. In August-September 1931, Nos 5275-94 were placed in store at Swindon (11), Caerphilly works (4), location unknown (5). In the summer of 1934, No 5275 was sent to Swindon works to emerge in August that year as No 7200. The remaining 19 stored locomotives were similarly treated between August and November being renumbered 7201-19 in the same sequence as their preceding 2-8-0T numbers.

The rebuilding process entailed bolting on rear extensions that lengthened the frames by 4' 1" to accommodate a trailer truck and enlargements to both bunker and rear water tank. As a result, coal capacity was doubled to six tons and water capacity increased from 1800 to 2500 gallons. These increases rendered an operational range not far short of tender locomotives, allowing the 2-8-2T to roam more broadly than the preceding 2-8-0T. The arrival of each new 2-8-2T accounted for a corresponding withdrawal of a member of "Aberdare" 2-6-0 Class 26xx, a type that dated from 1900/1.

No 7200 was in charge of an Up Class D freight (stopping at intermediate stations) which was hardly its intended type of duty. *Ref PG 37.*

Above: With continuing problems in the coal sector, the 2-8-0T to 2-8-2T conversion process was revived in September 1935. The next youngest of Class 42xx (numbers 5255 to 5274) which dated from 1925/ 6 were taken out of service between August 1935 and February 1936 for conversion, taking the numbers 7220-39 in the same sequence. The rear end modifications followed the pattern of Nos 7200-19 but the front end differed in retaining the straight running plate over the cylinders and square front drop end that had been standard with Class 42xx. When originally built Nos 5275 to 5294 (later Nos 7200-19) had introduced the raised platform over the cylinders and the curved drop end. On 29th September 1956, No 7238 headed an Up Class K pick-up goods southwards towards Oxford station – another case of under-exploitation of the type's potential. Comparison of No 7238 with the previous illustration clearly shows the front end differences, including the old style motion bar cross frame. *RCR Ref 7101-8100 (959)*

Opposite top: Class 72xx No 7228 (previously 2-8-0T Class 42xx No 5263) was standing with a rake of wagons in a siding at Wednesbury Central on 28th May 1960. This lengthy Class K train was more typical of the work for which these large machines had been intended. This locomotive was one of a pair from the 7220-39 series to be rebuilt a second time (dates unrecorded) by British Railways with raised platform over the cylinders and curved drop end (the other was No 7221). Despite installation of the more modern front end arrangements, these two locomotives retained the original style motion bar cross frame. *RCR Ref R14000-15099 (784).*

Opposite bottom: The third stage of the 42xx/ 72xx conversion programme commenced in August 1937 and by December 1939 had included a further fourteen locomotives before the exercise was terminated. The numbers 7240-53 were applied in order of conversion to older 2-8-0Ts that had been numbered between No 4202 (built January 1912) and No 4249 (built April 1916). In these cases, full front end re-styling was applied except for retention of the original motion bar cross frame. This view of No 7250 (ex-No 4219) at Swindon was dated 26th February 1939. The records show that the rebuilding was completed that month.

Their length made these impressive-looking locomotives curve-shy in certain sidings; those in preservation are Britain's largest surviving tank types. A Swindon drawing dated October 1941 has been traced that proposed conversion of Class 42xx into a 2-8-0 with a Standard No 1 boiler, which might have constituted a more effective improvement. *RCR Ref 1-1678 (133).*

Mainline freight

Opposite top: On 21st March 1960, No 5901 *Hazel Hall* had emerged from No 1 Tunnel (136 yards long), half a mile south east of Hockley station and was approaching Birmingham Snow Hill with an Up Class D express goods train i.e. with at least one-third of the vehicles vacuum-piped to the locomotive. The Hall looked grimy and judging by the escaping steam around the cylinders, was in run-down condition. However, it still had over four years of active life remaining, not being withdrawn until June 1964. *RCR Ref R14000-15099 (569).*

Opposite bottom: Class 8750 No 4646 was departing Birmingham Snow Hill with a Down freight on 21st March 1960. The train's composition was definitely eclectic, with a 5-plank wagon and tarpaulin in place behind the pannier tank, a pair of 16-ton mineral wagons, three tank wagons for petroleum products, another open wagon and then some loaded Macaws or bogie bolsters. This would appear to be a pick-up or transfer duty, although the headcode described a light engine working. *RCR Ref R14000-15099 (570).*

Immediately to the left of the locomotive is a BR-vintage covered van, then an ex-SR utility van, and then an ex-GWR Fruit D. The number cannot be discerned but it has been re-branded "Parcels Van/ Return to Old Oak Common". To the right stands the lofty Birmingham North Signal Box with a novel means of support to overcome space limitations. Immediately to the left of the box there appears to be siding for locomotive servicing, judging by the water column and the ash deposits in the four foot.

This page: On 9th October 1963, reasonably clean Modified Hall No 7927 *Willington Hall* has cleared Marsh Junction South with a Down Class E express freight on its way to the South West over the Bristol Relief Line. To the right stands St Philips Marsh locomotive depot, a double roundhouse shed with repair shops, that was home for around 140 locomotives, mainly mixed traffic 4-6-0s, 2-8-0s and tank locomotives. In the right background there is a collection of locomotives standing in the vicinity of the coal stage. The right foreground offers interesting detail of the shed environment. The water column is apparently located for the benefit of locomotives pausing on the Relief Line. In the siding there is a mobile crane (cab end closest) plus a pair of coaches – a Collett-era Composite and what appears to be a Toplight. They seem to have been transferred to departmental duties and stand alongside the shed's mess rooms; the repair shop is the building behind.

Bristol's express passenger engines were allocated to Bath Road shed, which was easily visible from the southern end of the Temple Meads platforms. *RCR Ref R16251-17500 (1199).*

Opposite top: The Great Central Railway's 2-8-0 Class 8K provided the basis for the standard heavy freight locomotive of the Railway Operating Division (Corps of Royal Engineers) during the First World War. Known as the RODs, after the conflict many were placed on short term loan with UK railway companies and in the 1920s four (GWR, LMS, LNER, LNWR) purchased examples outright while others were sold overseas. The tale of the RODs is complex but suffice to note here that 100 came into the ownership of the GWR (20 in 1919 and 80 in 1925). Fifty of the latter group did not last very long but the remainder were thoroughly overhauled and all acquired Swindon-design fittings while retaining their basic GCR styling and appearance.

Class 30xx (ROD) No 3026 was ordered by the UK Government in 1918 but not completed until 1919 by Nasmyth, Wilson Co Ltd (Maker's No 1282) as ROD No 1726. It remained in the UK and was placed on temporary loan with the GCR from late 1919 until August 1921. It was then stored at Royds Green, Leeds until purchase by the GWR in May 1925.

It is seen here passing Swindon on 16th May 1952 having been fully "Westernised" since the late 1920s with a type MB boiler (which included a copper firebox in place of the all-steel original), Swindon-style superheater, top feed, safety valve, chimney, smokebox door, plus short lap version of the standard piston valve. The train contains fitted vehicles but the head code correctly advises a Class E unfitted express freight as the GWR's RODs were never equipped with the vacuum brake. No 3026 worked until December 1954. *RCR Ref 2199 to 3948 (910).*

Opposite bottom: Class 30xx roamed widely throughout the GWR system by virtue of their Blue route availability. Here No 3017 was trundling behind Newton Abbot West Signal Box on 2nd May 1953 with a through Up Class H unfitted freight train. This engine was built by North British Locomotive Co Ltd, Hyde Park works (Maker's No 22124) in April 1919 and purchased by the GWR in brand new condition the following July. In due course it received the full Westernisation treatment and worked until October 1956.

The pavement between railway property and the roadway to the right of the picture was well trodden by enthusiasts as it afforded a grandstand view of all the complex comings and goings. Summer Saturdays would ensure a bumper crowd but on this occasion the audience is small. *Ref PG 265.*

Above: Dick Riley's description of this photograph cryptically states "4052 Tn Llantihangel 1/6/53" but the location is actually near Llanvihangel (Mon) on the Newport-Hereford line. The train is a northbound Class F unfitted express freight, carrying steel products loaded mainly on Macaws and the like. The train locomotive is extremely dirty Star Class No 4052 *Princess Beatrice* which had been rebuilt in April 1939 with new inside and outside cylinders, and so Castle-style steam pipes. Only thirteen of the class acquired this feature. No 4052 was withdrawn in June 1953 so this might even have been this grand old engine's final revenue-earning duty. The identity of the banking locomotive is not recorded.
RCR Ref 2199 to 3948 (1144).

Class 2884 No 3843 on a London-bound Class H unfitted freight near Tilehurst on 17th September 1955. The first 20-odd wagons are laden with coal while the remainder appears to be general freight. 0-6-2T No 5639 is passing bunker-first on the Down line. *RCR Ref 6101-7100 (516).*

Above: Churchward's final design, 2-8-0 Class 47xx, is today regarded as having been largely confined to nocturnal activities and so rarely seen at work during the daylight hours. How this myth came about is unclear but it is confounded by copious photographic evidence (and by the compiler's treasured memories). The notion of "daylight scarcity" probably had more to do with their only ever having been nine of these magnificent beasts (at least for the time being).

Here, grimy No 4701 is coming to a halt on the through road at Totnes with a Down Class H unfitted freight on 14th June 1952. The cloud of steam behind the 47's tender indicates that a banking engine is standing in the platform loop, waiting to back out on to the Down main and buffer up to the Toad in readiness for the assault on Rattery bank.

Just ahead of No 4701, 0-4-2T Class 14xx No 1470 stands with an auto coach at the platform forming the branch service to Ashburton. This locomotive was the regular Ashburton branch passenger locomotive and in its early BR neo-LNWR lined black livery, it looks considerably smarter than the 2-8-0. In later years it was reduced to plain black, never receiving the lined green that so suited these cheerful little locomotives.

The Ashburton line skirted the River Dart and came close to that part of the river favoured by students from nearby Dartington Hall Arts Centre for nude swimming. The Ashburton auto coach was reputed to suffer from weaker springs on the river side – but this is surely apocryphal. *Ref PG 194.*

Right: With the Teign Estuary in the right background, No 5967 *Bickmarsh Hall* is nearing Hackney yard, Newton Abbot at the head of a lengthy Class H unfitted goods train on 14th March 1955. *Ref PG 512.*

Opposite top: On 30th April 1955 No 7907 *Hart Hall* was confidently tackling Dainton East with a Down Class D express goods, banked by 2-6-2T No 5150 which has yet to come into view. Four of the first six vehicles are cattle wagons. *Ref PG 540.*

Opposite bottom: A Down Class H unfitted goods headed by 2-8-0 No 2843 was near Coombe Fishacre descending Dainton west bank on 20th April 1957. The GWR and BR (WR) extracted full value from this superb design. This locomotive was built in November 1912 and received a front end rebuild with outside steam pipes in April 1947. Withdrawal of the 28s commenced in April 1958 and No 2843 was taken out of service in June 1959. *Ref PG 1012.*

This page, top: On a gloomy cold 21st March 1959, Class 28xx No 2807 is drawing out of Exeter St David's with a Down Class H unfitted goods. The prototype for this class appeared in 1903 and No 2807, as part of the first production run, entered service in October 1905. The 28s formed the backbone of long distance freight operations until the end of steam under BR (WR). This example was modified with curved front drop end and outside steam pipes in November 1936, and when withdrawn in March 1963 was the oldest GWR 2-8-0 remaining in service. After an extended sojourn at Barry, it returned to work in preserved form.

Eleven years on from nationalisation, this view is redolent of the GWR with only the diesel shunter present to spoil the effect. *Ref PG 1773.*

Photographers generally preferred Exeter St Davids as that station saw more action, including that provided by the "other" railway/ region, while Exeter St Thomas one mile to the south was a much more modest establishment. No 5904 *Kelham Hall* was heading a Down Class C fully fitted parcels or perishables train under the now sadly removed Brunel–style overall roof on 15th February 1958. *Ref PG 1274.*

25

Opposite top: Between Clerks Tunnel (58 yards) and Parsons Tunnel (513 yards), 2-6-0 Class 73xx No 7339 (previously No 9317) was heading a Class D express freight on 15th June 1958. *Ref PG 1366.*

Opposite bottom: On the western side of Dainton tunnel on 31st July 1959, No 6814 *Enborne Grange* has commenced its careful descent with a Class E express goods. The engine looks tidily presented, complemented by the 3500-gallon tender that appeared more at home with this class than the larger variety. The fireman looks relaxed and the safety valve is feathering steam. This suggests that the banking locomotive, Prairie No 4105 which has yet to emerge from the tunnel, did most of the work on the climb. Where cattle wagons were included in mixed freight trains, it was normal practice for them to be marshalled next to the locomotive to minimise the effect of coupling snatch, and so that the locomotive crew was close at hand to provide succour to animals in distress. Beyond providing refuge for banking locomotives, the sidings appear to be falling into disuse by this date. *Ref PG 2015.*

Above: By the late 1950s, 2-10-0 BR Standard Class were regularly evident in the South West on goods services, and on summer Saturday passenger "extras". On 22nd July 1959, No 92209 had cleared Dainton tunnel with an Up Class C fully fitted express freight. By then the ranks of ex-GWR Class 28xx were thinning but these tragically short-lived 2-10-0s were worthy successors. *Ref PG 1980.*

Opposite top: Collett 2-6-0 No 7333 at the head of a Class B Goods emerges from Dainton tunnel on 29th July 1959 with the first of its two climbs on the journey to Plymouth completed. At this stage the banking locomotive, reported as 2-6-2T Class 5101 No 5196, would still be working hard on the other side of the summit and had yet to enter the tunnel.

The rationale for certain aspects of the GWR's locomotive construction policy during the 1930s is hard to understand, as with the case of No 7333 which was built as No 9311 in March 1932. It was one of a batch of 20 locomotives produced as a modernised version of Churchward's original design with screw reverse, side-window cab, outside steam pipes, a slight increase in boiler pitch, and an increase in weight of around 3 tons. These changes placed this batch in the red category for route availability which reduced their scope of operations. Whether these 20 engines were really needed is questionable. The original moguls were useful engines but were sometimes given duties that tested the capacity of their No 4 boilers. By then there was a need for a smaller wheeled 4-6-0 carrying a No 1 boiler, as originally envisaged by Churchward in his standardisation plan, which was eventually satisfied by the Grange Class of 1936. No 93xx series was modified in 1956-9 to reduce weight and thus enable Blue route availability. No 9311 was so treated in June 1957 and concurrently renumbered 7333; it was withdrawn in October 1963. *Ref PG 2011.*

Opposite bottom: Built in December 1920, Churchward Mogul No 6301 was still able to give a good account of itself as it arrived at Plymouth North Road on 2nd January 1960, heading a lengthy van train working under Class H head code. No 6301 remained in service until October 1962; these useful 2-6-0s became extinct as a class in October 1964. *Ref PG 2197.*

This page: Easy work for a thoroughbred. Class 28xx No 2811 passes Old Oak Common East on 20th August 1955. According to the headcode, officially this is a Class D wholly, or at least one-third, vacuum-braked express goods train which seems a generous categorisation given the load, but weight and length were not determinants in the classification system. This locomotive, built in November 1905 as one of the first production batch, was modernised by fitting of outside steam pipes and curved front drop end in February 1943, and stayed in service until October 1959. *Ref RCR 6101-7100 (323).*

Chapter 2
Parcels

The generic term "parcels" covered trains that conveyed a wide range of merchandise, including foodstuffs, trunks and cases, industrial machinery, motor vehicles and so forth. Essentially, their role was to move cargoes that could not be comfortably accommodated in a passenger service although some surprising items appeared in the latter. (The compiler recalls in the mid-1950s alighting at Cheltenham Malvern Road from a passenger service from Exeter and helping the guard to manhandle a recalcitrant sheep out of the van space adjacent to his compartment).

Parcels trains typically embraced great variety in their composition with bogie vehicles, plus six and four wheelers, spiced with a cosmopolitan flavour through representatives of the other companies. This theme flourished after nationalisation and expansion of the general user principle. To some degree, the GWR had favoured the dedication of vehicles to specific routes and marked them accordingly, a practice that continued after 1948.

However, in 1966 a maroon-liveried Hawksworth Passenger Brake Van branded "Paddington and Birkenhead" spotted at Calstock in Cornwall exemplified the relaxation of this discipline in later years.

A strong Great Western flavour persisted in the composition of these services to the end of the steam era. Passenger Brake Vans of the Collett and Hawksworth eras were usually present, and even the occasional ageing Toplight. In the transit of merchandise, Siphons G regularly predominated thereby fulfilling a general utility role long after retirement from milk duties. The slatted sides and thus fresh air ventilation of these versatile vehicles made them ideal for a wide variety of perishable cargoes, subject to their having first satisfied stringent regulations concerning internal cleanliness. Loads included apples, asparagus, beans, brussels sprouts, broccoli, flowers, plums, potatoes, strawberries etc harvested according to season in the Channel Islands, the Isles of Scilly, Cornwall, Devon,

Although Dick Riley started railway photography about 1937, the limited capacity of his camera equipment meant that his pre-war images of trains on the move were comparatively few. Here he has succeeded in capturing No 6879 *Overton Grange* passing Stafford Road shed, Wolverhampton on 25th June 1939 with two horse boxes coupled immediately behind the locomotive. Neither can be positively identified but the vertical body end suggests that the first was from Diagram N16 of 1937. The head lamps indicate that this was actually an express passenger train.

No 6879, the last built of a highly regarded class, was then a month old. One hundred mixed traffic 4-6-0s were created using parts recycled from withdrawn 2-6-0s of Class 43xx and it seems likely that this programme would have continued but for the outbreak of war just over two months later. The eighty Granges belatedly filled a gap in Churchward's locomotive standardisation programme; the smaller-boilered Manors that also utilised 43xx parts proved rather less distinguished. *Ref RCR 1-1698 (510).*

Somerset, west Wales, the Vale of Evesham and many other rural areas. Even after this traffic had defected to the roads, some Siphons proved long-lived as with most of their ventilation slats plated over and in unfriendly "rail blue", they could still be seen on newspaper trains at Paddington into the 1980s.

Other members of the non-passenger fleet were also present – Stowage vans, 4- and 6-wheel Siphons C, Fish vans and Bloaters, Fruits plus the larger C & D versions (the latter re-designated Pasfruit in recognition of their eligibility to work in passenger trains), Horse Boxes and Beetles (latter for prize cattle), Scenery vans and Covered Carriage Trucks. Parcels trains embraced the full

panoply of the GWR's variegated "brown vehicles", not forgetting those that were not actually brown (e.g. milk tankers) and also fitted departmental vehicles such as Cordon gas carriers.

The diversity of motive power deployed from panniers through to 4-6-0s added to the interest. There would be pauses at minor stations to collect seasonal produce as witnessed personally on a summer's Sunday evening in 1956 when locally grown violets were loaded at Starcross. The motive power was sparkling No 7018 *Drysllwyn Castle,* under road test following its experimental fitting with a double chimney, and coupled to a self-weighing tender.

On 24th July 1957, Churchward No 6319 was running into Gwinear Road with a Down Class C parcels service showing the mixture of rolling stock that made this type of train so interesting. Immediately behind the tender is a 6-wheel milk tanker being returned empty in readiness for the next journey "up-country", followed by an ex-SR 4-wheel utility van, a closed van and then an ex-GWR Passenger Brake Van. The home signal mounted on the footbridge signifies that an Up service is due. Small prairie No 4505 stands in the far platform that served the Helston line. Its train, most probably a 2-coach B-set, is out of shot; presumably it awaits connection with the Up arrival *PG Ref 1131.*

BR 2-10-0 Class 9F No 92226 is in the typical work-stained, grimy condition that afflicted so many of this class but which never detracted from the impressive appearance. This Class C working is described as a Down Fish near Tigley Signal Box, ascending Rattery bank on 9th August 1959. The first vehicle seems to be an LMS Period I (Hughes era) Corridor Full Brake, possibly of Diagram 1778, followed by eight wagons including a fitted open that looks rather out of place, then an ex-GWR PBV and finally what might be a pair of ex-LNER passenger vehicles. *Ref PG 2065.*

Twenty days later on 30th August 1959 and again in the vicinity of Tigley Signal Box, possibly the same service as that depicted in the previous view looks rather different in the hands of Mogul No 6341. This time there are six 4-wheel vans leading, followed by the distinctive outline of the inevitable ex-GWR PBV and then further bogie vehicles. *Ref PG 2089.*

Parsels

There is no record of the date of this view but the location appears to be Acton West with an Up Class C working. No 7813 *Freshford Manor*'s tender is one of the ten 3500-gallon "Intermediate" type numbered 2374-83 built in 1925/6. The train comprises a Fruit C followed by four Fruits D, an LMS Full Brake, a Collett All Third coach of the immediate pre-Sunshine series, an earlier bow-ended Collett PBV (possibly Diagram K40), and finally what might be a pair of inside-framed Siphons G. The Fruit C and its adjacent companion appear to have been recently repainted. *RCR Ref 7101-8100 (346).*

Above: The seventy members of 2-6-2T Class 61xx spent most of their careers on various duties in the London Division until dispersal to points further away following dieselisation of Thames Valley passenger services. On 22nd August 1959, 2-6-2T No 6161 working under Category C headcode (fully fitted parcels train) was approaching Kensington Olympia on a service from Reading. The composition was a BR Mark 1 Full Brake, possibly a Mink, then a Hawksworth PBV (Diagram K45 or K46) and finally two more BR Full Brakes. The Hawksworth PBV, rather cleaner than the other bogie vehicles, appears to carry route branding but the details are too distant to be discerned. *RCR Ref 14000-15099 (187).*

Top: On 22nd May 1961, No 1006 *County of Cornwall* was heading an Up Class C perishables at Doublebois between Bodmin Road and Liskeard. Modernity is evident as following the two leading vehicles (an inside-framed Siphon G and a Hawksworth Brake Third of Diagram D131 or D133), there are a pair of BR-built General Utility Vehicles and then a Mark 1 Full Brake. The next vehicle cannot be identified but there is then a closed van followed by three 6-wheel milk tankers. The term "perishable" would seem to embrace a wide variety of cargos. *Ref PG 2531.*

Bottom: Apart from the twelve members of the aircraft series (Nos 5071 to 5082), only three Castles carried names with direct military connotations (Nos 4016, 4037 and 5017). The last of these renamings concerned No 5017 when in April 1954 *St. Donats Castle* became *The Gloucestershire Regiment 28th 61st* to commemorate that unit's participation in The Battle of the Imjin River in the Korean War. This was an action fought during three nights that cost over 90% of the regimental strength in soldiers killed or taken prisoner, and which earned the United States Presidential Citation.

No 5017, for long a resident (unsurprisingly) of Gloucester was often rostered to work the *Cheltenham Spa Express* between there and Paddington but on 29th August 1959 it was heading the more mundane Class C 2.21 pm Down Parcels when photographed near Old Oak Common. A Fruit D is immediately behind the tender, then a BR General Utility Vehicle, a BR Mark 1 PBV and then another Fruit D; the remainder cannot be discerned. The passenger rake to the left includes a bow-ended Collett-era Composite (possible Diagrams are E127, E132 or E139).

No 5017's name plate was unusual in being formed of a single black-backed panel above the centre splasher in a style used only once before with No 4016 *The Somerset Light Infantry (Prince Albert's)*. The Glosters' regimental badge was mounted in brass on the splasher face. *RCR Ref 14000-15099 (202).*

Rather grimy No 4056 *Princess Margaret* approaches Teignmouth on 19th July 1956. The following year this locomotive was maintained in smarter condition by Bristol Bath Road in acknowledgement of its celebrity role as the last Star in service. Dick Riley's notes describe this train as a Down fish, apparently returning for more. The first vehicle is a four wheeled van following by a brake van of non-GWR origin (note the ducket) and then what seems to be a GWR brake coach. Unfortunately, there is no further information on how the remainder of the train was made up. *RCR Ref 7101-8100 (659).*

No 4992 *Crosby Hall* has cleared Aller Junction and is vigorously attacking Dainton East on 20th July 1963. By that summer, the ranks of steam had substantially thinned in the West and searching out 4-6-0s on mainline duties required patience, in marked contrast to the bounty of previous years. There is still a comforting GWR element in the train with a Siphon J behind the tender while the fifth vehicle is a Hawksworth PBV. At the tail there appears to be two BR Mark 1s passenger brakes and a BR general utility van. *Ref PG 3307.*

The location is Moreton sidings about one mile east of Didcot and the date is 4th July 1953. Star Class No 4062 *Malmesbury Abbey* is approaching with a Down parcels service. By then there were few of Churchward's masterpiece remaining in service and their work was largely reduced to parcels and secondary mainline passenger trains. (A body of opinion four years later held that No 4056 was still good enough to haul *The Bristolian*, sadly never attempted).

Little can be seen of the train's composition but there are at least two Siphons to the right of the signal post and a GWR PBV around about number six in the consist. The density and diversity of freight traffic in the mid-1950s is emphasised by the volume of wagons standing in the extensive sidings on the Up side. The fine array of signals with the distant off shows that the Star has a clear road on the Down main, about to be confirmed by the attendant ATC ramp. *RCR Ref 3949-4941 (35).*

Same day and location as the previous photograph but in this case Modified Hall No 7915 *Mere Hall* is proceeding under caution with another Down parcels working. The train reporting number chalked on the smokebox cannot be explained as "291" does not appear in the lists for either 1952 or 1953. The vehicle behind the tender is unidentifiable but the next (partially obscured) might be a Monster. Further along there are a couple of GWR PBVs and some Siphons. View of the sidings to the left is obscured by the passing BR Mark 1 stock of *The Bristolian. RCR Ref 3949-4941 (38).*

Dick Riley's notes advise that this is an Up Salop vans train at Banbury on 30th April 1956, in the hands of Didcot-based No 6910 *Gossington Hall.* In order from the front, the part of the composition that can be seen is:- BR Mark I Full Brake/ ex-LMS Period III Corridor Full Brake (possibly Diagram 1854)/ Fruit D/ BR Mark I Full Brake/ possibly ex-LMS Period I Corridor Full Brake/ unidentified/ ex-GWR PBV/ outside framed Siphon G/ unidentified. *RCR Ref 5001-6100 (906).*

Above: Every GWR album should include a King which can be a challenge in a book about non-passenger services. In BR's 8P power category, this class was unique in remaining almost exclusively on express passenger duties to the end of their careers. Apart from *King George V*, No 6026 was perhaps the only class member whose name was readily identifiable by virtue of the absence of a numerical suffix in the monarchical title (a feature shared only by No 6029 until its transition from *King Stephen* to *King Edward VIII* in May 1936). On 4th August 1950, No 6026 *King John* with its Class C headlamps looking rather out of place was heading the 3.48 pm Bristol-Plymouth parcels service through Wellington, Somerset. The train comprises what appears to be an ex-LNER 6-wheel carriage truck, a standard ex-LNER closed van, an inside-framed Siphon G, a 4-wheel ex-Southern utility van, an ex-LMS Full Brake, a GWR PBV, an ex-Southern utility van and then a GWR PBV or passenger coach while those to the left of the post are indistinguishable.

No 6026 had a probably unique connection with Cornwall which as every schoolboy knew was territory forbidden to the Kings on account of their double-red route classification. In the late 1950s a motive power crisis caused by a concurrence of diesel failures at Plymouth enforced the use of No 6026 on a service to Truro. On arrival in the far west, the illegal immigrant was deported immediately light engine to the correct side of the River Tamar. *Ref PG 668.*

Opposite top: Wrong line working on Sunday 15th July 1956 as the other would appear to be occupied for engineering work - note the basic protection of a solitary flag vertical against the running rail. No 1011 *County of Chester* approaches with a Down Class C parcels train near Mannamead Signal Box, halfway between Lipson Vale Halt and Mutley Tunnel, Plymouth. The train comprises two ex-LMS Full Brakes (the second in "blood & custard livery"), three closed vans, and a GWR PBV bringing up the rear. *Ref RCR 7101-8100 (589).*

No 5003 *Lulworth Castle* **was departing Penzance on 12th July 1956 with the 2.00 pm Class C perishables. The train comprises three PBV/ full Brakes of differing origins (ex-LMS/ BR Mark 1/ ex-GWR), an ex-SR 4-wheel utility van, and what appear to be a pair of ex-LNER vans – six vehicles together representing the Big Four and BR.** *Ref RCR 7101-8100 (529).*

Mention of Swindon-built 2-cylinder mixed traffic 4-6-0s automatically evokes thoughts of Halls, Granges, Manors and Counties while overlooking British Railways Type 4 Class 75xxx, a design that played an important role in the evolution of Great Western design practice. From their introduction in 1938, the Manors were noted for their erratic steaming in stark contrast to engines fitted with the Standard No 1 boiler. Perhaps because of use on secondary duties, the type's malaise went unacknowledged but it was definitely curious that the matter was not properly investigated until 1952. This followed comparative testing at Swindon against a new Class 75xxx which achieved a maximum steaming rate of 19,200 lb per hour. The Manor was then tried and found to be barely capable of reaching 10,000 lb per hour. Irony and embarrassment lay in both types, similar in size and nominal power output, having been designed and built at Swindon. The exercise led to corrective work on the Manors which transformed their performance.

No 75001 was on an Up Class C parcels working on 1st August 1959 in the classic Great Western setting of Sonning cutting. In the opening comments to this chapter, reference was made to the increasing cosmopolitan composition of parcels trains in BR days and here is a perfect example. There is a Southern 4-wheel utility van, three PBVs (of BR, LMS and LNER origin), a couple of ex-LNER closed vans but nothing in the entire consist that can definitely confirmed as of GWR heritage. Perhaps No 75001, a member of perhaps the most attractive of the British Railway Standard classes, deserves accordance of that status at least on an honorary basis. *RCR Ref 12901-13999 (1073).*

Chapter 3
Dedicated Trains

While a wide variety of farm produce reached London and other markets by "parcel" workings, certain cargoes were transported in sufficient volume to require their own special services that would be now referred to as "block trains". As a seasonal vegetable, broccoli could not justify provision of its own rolling stock so practice was to employ suitably cleaned cattle wagons. Farmers delivered the vegetables to collection points, especially in Cornwall, for loading by hand into cattle wagons marshalled into special trains.

In contrast, shipment of substantial volumes of milk was a year-round obligation that required a complex transportation and processing infrastructure prior to loading into purpose-designed railway vehicles. Movement of milk in churns had traditionally used Siphons but this mode had largely given way to short-lived 4-wheel tank wagons before World War 2. The need for a more stable running vehicle soon led to the 6-wheel version that stayed in service until road transport took over.

Up milk trains were a distinctive daily feature of afternoon/ evening services and their comparatively short length disguised their weight as a laden 6-wheel milk tanker approximated that of a bogie coach. Mainline locomotive power was engaged on these services, typically Castle, County, Hall and Grange classes while west of Newton Abbot, 2-8-0s were often used. Each train included a Passenger Brake Van and it was common for empty Cordons to be added at the rear for the first stage of their journey back to Swindon Gas Works for replenishment.

The Granges with their 5' 8" driving wheels were ideally suited for services over the Cornish switchback, including the broccoli specials. No 6869 *Resolven Grange*, carrying Class D head code, was engaged in assembling stock for such a service at Marazion on 19th March 1960. *RCR Ref 14000-15099 (542).*

Western Region non-passenger trains

Dedicated Trains

Opposite top: This scene at Ponsandane, a little to the east of Penzance, on 9th April 1960 illustrates the simplicity of the broccoli delivery and loading process, prior to despatch to London. It is not clear why two cases are on the roof of the wagon. Motive power: - (left) Ferguson TE20 introduced 1946, overall plain grey livery that was not dissimilar to GWR freight stock, Registration No. OAF 140 and (right) 50 hp Fordson Major introduced in 1952 and probably in standard blue livery with orange wheels and radiator grill, Registration No PRL 856. (Both tractors were registered in Cornwall). *RCR Ref 14000-15099 (652).*

Opposite bottom: An amusing aspect of watching trains in the 1950s was that particular engines seemed to turn up time and again, whatever the location, and personal recollections place Castles *Carew* and *Clun* in this category. For Dick Riley, No 4083 *Abbotsbury Castle* (and also pannier tank No 3635) were recurring subjects of his photographic attention. Built in May 1925, No 4083 was the first of the second production batch of Castles, remaining in more or less original condition throughout its career except for the provision of the Hawksworth tender, as shown here. On 9th April 1960, this splendid veteran was nearing its 35th birthday; withdrawal came in December 1961 with breaking up taking place at Swindon.

No 4083 is preparing to leave Ponsandane with the Class D express freight train (at least one-third fitted and piped to the locomotive) that was being loaded in the previous view. The significance of broccoli and other traffic for the railway can be judged by the amount of stock in the yard. On the left behind the BR brake van can be seen a yard shunter in the form of an 0-6-0PT Class 94xx. *RCR Ref 14000-15099 (660).*

This page: Class 94xx No 9433 with companion gig working as yard shunter at Ponsandane on 9th April 1960. *RCR Ref 14000-15099 (654).*

Top: No 4083 has now moved a little forward but has yet to gain the main line as No 6875 *Hindford Grange* with the 1.20 pm from Penzance passes by with the Castle's crew looking on. The Grange's train comprises four BR Mark 1 coaches plus an inside-framed siphon on the rear. *RCR Ref 14000-15099 (656).*

Middle: Nine miles west of St Austell and near Probus & Lodock, No 4931 *Hanbury Hall* has had an easy journey so far with this milk train. The load comprises two tankers, a Passenger Brake Van and a pair of Cordons (a nine tank Diagram DD4 leading and a twin tank Diagram DD5 following). The gas tanks probably started their journey at either Penzance or Truro. More 6-wheel tankers will be added at various collecting points as this train proceeds eastwards. *RCR Ref 6101-7100 (70).*

Above: With milk bound for Kensington on 5th July 1955, 4-6-0 No 1018 *County of Leicester* climbs Treverrin bank (1 in 62 at its steepest), roughly mid-way between Par and Lostwithiel. The train appears to comprise eight milk tankers plus the inevitable PBV. *Ref RCR 6101-7100 (40).*

Opposite bottom: No 1002 County of Berks leaving Lostwhithiel with the 6.20 pm milk from Penzance on 7th July 1955. *RCR Ref 6101-7100 (66).*

Above: Milk depots were also located away from main line routes and these were served by dedicated branch line services as in the case of Lifton on the Launceston branch, about four miles to the east of the terminus. On 15th July 1956, small prairie No 4590 was approaching Laira Junction, signalled for the route through Mutley to Plymouth North Road with the daily milk shipment contained in three tank wagons. Despite this being a branch orientated service, the engine is working under Class C Express parcels etc head code. The Passenger Brake Van is a Toplight (Diagram K19 or K22). *RCR Ref 7101-8100 (593).*

Opposite top: On 29th May 1957, No 6986 *Rydal Hall* leads No 3822 into the tunnel having climbed Dainton west bank with a comparatively modest load of six tankers, plus PBV and a Cordon. *Ref PG1089.*

Opposite bottom: On 18th August 1961, No 6928 *Underley Hall* was in charge of an Up milk train near Tigley Signal Box comprising nine 6-wheel tankers and a Hawksworth passenger brake van. The estimated weight of this train is around 300 tons which was at the 300 ton weight limit for a Hall unassisted over the south Devon banks east of Hemerdon. *Ref PG2706.*

Left: The 12.20 pm milk from Penzance has reached Exeter St David's in the care of No 6934 *Beachamwell Hall* on 15th July 1955 and is almost at Red Cow Crossing, immediately to the east of the station. *RCR Ref 6101-7100 (256).*

Bottom: The most picturesque collection point for milk was possibly Hemyock at the end of the 7-mile Culm Valley branch from Tiverton Junction. By tortuous curves this rural route wended its way through Coldharbour, Uffculme, Culmstock and Whitehall to terminate at the diminutive Hemyock station with the dairy immediately beyond. Class 14xx was the largest permitted over this restricted route where progress was inevitably slow. On 3rd August 1953, No 1405 was about to depart for the junction, with five milk tankers and ex-Barry Railway 51' Brake Third No W263W. This short bogie coach was built in 1920 and remained in service until October 1962. *Ref PG 338.*

On 23rd July 1958, No 1449 had arrived at the Hemyock platform (on the Down side) at Tiverton Junction and detached the brake coach. It had then crossed the mainline and shunted the five milk tankers on to the rear of a semi-fast Up service (headed by 2-6-0 No 6358) for the next stage of the journey to London. *RCR Ref 11801-12900 (809).*

West Ealing sidings was an assembly point for empty milk tankers after discharge at the Milk Marketing Board's establishment at Addison Road, Kensington. On 11th April 1955, No 4917 *Crosswood Hall* was setting out for Whitland, Carmarthenshire with 17 empty tankers plus PBV. *RCR Ref 5001-6100 (998).*

No 4941 *Llangedwyn Hall* was on the Down Main in Sonning cutting on 19th July 1959 with a return working of milk empties. Judging by the length of the train, and the presence of two PBVs plus some vans that might be Fruits, this seems to be a vehicle combination that would have formed two up workings the previous day. *RCR Ref 12901-1399 (1049).*

Near Hungerford on 7th July 1956, eleven milk tankers were being returned to the West Country by No 6921 *Borwick Hall. RCR Ref 7101-8100 (385).*

Chapter 4
Local Goods

The Great Western, possibly the first enterprise to operate a petrol-powered omnibus in Britain, had a fleet of 108 vehicles by 1929. Following legislative changes, the fleet was distributed among independently-owned regional companies. The GWR took shares in those bodies and by 1933 had withdrawn from direct participation in the bus market. From inception, it had been practice for GWR omnibuses additionally to carry goods and parcels but the service's popularity soon engendered capacity problems that necessitated creation of a road vehicle fleet solely for movement of goods. The company had always used horse-drawn wagons for collection and

distribution from its rail-served goods depots but the speed and flexibility of the motor lorry opened up significant commercial opportunities.

GWR motor lorries were soon covering areas within a 20-mile radius of goods depots and later worked further afield. Out of this developed a cartage service where point-to-point deliveries were completed without recourse to movements by rail, and a lorry fleet that had comprised 392 in 1923 grew to 2,324 by 1937. Statistical comparison among the Big Four reveals that the GWR embraced mechanisation of its road goods fleet most rapidly and by 1937 accounted for 24%

In the 21st Century, the role of the branch (Class K) goods train as an integral part of the rural economy and local transport network is easily forgotten. On 27th February 1959, a pannier tank (believed to be Class 8750 No 3796) was passing through a sylvan setting between Brimley and Heathfield on the Moretonhampstead branch, returning to Newton Abbot with the daily goods working. The train appears to comprise nine wagons, probably all empty, plus the Toad. The vehicle types suggest the cargoes they had delivered: farm machinery on the flatwagon behind the locomotive; general merchandise in the six closed vans; house coal in the two opens. Of the two main settlements served, Bovey Tracey was easily accessible by road but Moretonhampstead, 12 miles from Newton up on the edge of Dartmoor, was quite remote and reached by a poor road. The branch provided an important service to that small town until its closure to passengers in February 1959, and to goods in April 1964. *Ref PG 1755.*

of all railway-owned lorries, but only 12% of all horse-drawn wagons (and only 6% of shunting horses!).

The efficiency of GWR road services helped sustain localised rail traffic but could not avoid the fact that to some degree the company was competing with itself while educating potential new hauliers and existing customers about the advantages of road over rail. With nationalisation, the Big Four's road transport activities were hived off and combined in the newly formed British Road Services. The migration of local traffic, ironically initially stimulated by the GWR's pre-war enterprise, continued under BR Western Region. The declining fortunes of short distance rail freight services over trunk routes and branch lines inevitably made them a rationalisation target under the Beeching Plan.

Diminishing utilisation at small stations often quite lavishly equipped to handle small and large goods items (e.g. the goods shed, office, cattle dock, sidings and cranage) did not necessarily

detract from a service that played a community role. Certain branch termini satisfied important local needs by virtue of their location – in Devon, Moretonhampstead and Princetown were cogent examples – but in the period covered by this work their futures were sealed. Usually, passenger services went first which could be inconvenient for residual travellers. However, this measure did reduce costs as lines could then be worked as long sidings on the one-engine-in-steam principle thus eking out an existence before total closure. In a very few lucky cases this process yielded the dividend of a second life in preservation. The Ashburton branch was a good example where the infrastructure's survival as far as Buckfastleigh boosted start-up of the Dart Valley Railway.

Branch and local goods trains were the natural habitat of prairies and panniers and their eradication more or less coincided with the end of steam. Fortunately, these long-departed activities have been well preserved on film.

In contrast to the Devonian idyll, transfer freight movements in the London area could be complex and involve substantial loads. In this case No 8756 of Old Oak Common (to which depot the first batch of Class 8750 was allocated when new) is drawing its train from the Victoria branch out on to the West London line, bound for Addison Road (now Kensington Olympia) and points further south. The Riley notes indicate that this train started from Old Oak Common; it comprises five flat (Conflat) wagons carrying containers, three closed vans, seven more loaded Conflats, and four or five more closed vans. The ducket-equipped brake van is obviously of non-GWR origin (Toads were restricted use vehicles) which underlines the interregional nature of this working; the ST headcode indicates that the train is bound for New Kew Junction and likely one of the Southern Region yards in South London.

Prior to 1931, open wagons and match trucks had been typically used for insulated and ordinary containers. The Conflat type (Diagram H6) introduced that year was specifically designed for this traffic and construction continued through Diagrams H7 to H11, concluding in BR days by when there were 2,025 in service. Insulated containers were used especially for meat and it may be assumed that this train includes empties returning from Smithfield market.

The West London line was (and remains) an important means of circumventing the capital on a north-south axis. It was heavily used in GWR days by goods trains, plus a sprinkling of commuter services and inter-company passenger traffic. The pannier tank is almost abreast of North Pole Junction Signal Box, a London & North Western Railway structure erected at the boundary between the end of that company's line from Willesden Junction and commencement of the West London Railway which was jointly owned by the GWR and LNWR from there to West Kensington. Ownership of the section onwards to Clapham Junction was shared by the GWR, LNWR plus the London & South Western and London, Brighton & South Coast railways. *RCR Ref 14000-15099 (61).*

Dick Riley preferred mainline and shed scenes so his views of obscure freight-only branch lines were scarce. On 20th July 1960, he captured small prairie No 5552 shunting at the terminus of the Newham branch on the quay adjoining the Truro River. This line, which was 2¼ miles long, trailed in off the Truro-Falmouth branch immediately after Penwithers Junction on the Cornish main line.

The Newham branch was opened for passengers and goods in April 1855 by the standard gauge West Cornwall Railway and followed a generally U-shaped course to reach the terminus from the south. Traffic development was hampered by break-of-gauge with the broad gauge Cornwall Railway and in financial straits, the WCR was acquired by the "Associated Companies" group (GWR, Bristol & Exeter Railway and South Devon Railway) in January 1866. Newham passenger services had already been withdrawn in 1863 but goods-only status was retained until complete closure in November 1971. *RCR Ref 15000-18250 (55).*

Local Goods

Opposite top: Newton Abbot-based Class 5101 No 5178 was in charge of a modestly-sized Class K pick-up goods consisting of eight goods vehicles plus the obligatory Toad, near Milber just to the east of Aller Junction on 13th April 1957. The train is destined for the Torbay branch and comprises two 5-plank open wagons which judging by their corrugated metal ends are not of GWR origin, an ex-Southern Railway van, then what might be a pair of Minks, an unidentifiable van, and then a pair of open wagons. With a nominal tractive effort of 24,300 lb, this is an undemanding duty for the prairie. *Ref PG 999.*

Opposite bottom: Peter Gray describes this train as a Down freight at Laira hauled by pannier tank No 4679 on 29th April 1961. However, it can be surmised that it is a transfer duty from Tavistock Junction sidings that has been signalled for the left hand Down line at Laira Junction, being destined for the North Quay branch. Despite the Class J empty wagon head code, the three tank wagons must surely be loaded as is the timber-bodied open wagon. Presumably, accurate train description was considered unnecessary on this short, local journey. *Ref PG 2512.*

Below: This Class K branch goods from Newton Abbot to Ashburton has cleared the tunnel and is descending Dainton East on its return working on 25th March 1954. At least fourteen wagons can be detected in the train so possibly traffic had been collected from Totnes as well as from the three stations with siding facilities on the branch. Newton Abbot depot had a habit of using specific locomotives for the Ashburton line – auto-fitted 0-4-2T Class 14xx No 1470 for passenger duties, and 2-6-2T Class 44xx No 4401 for freight, as seen here.

There were only eleven examples of 4' 1½" Class 44xx (dating from1904-6) before the similar Class 45xx (with 4' 7½" driving wheels) was built in greater numbers from 1906 onwards. The earlier version became extinct in 1955 with the withdrawal of No 4401 in October 1954. Another duty with which Class 44xx was closely associated over many years was working mixed and passenger trains over the steeply graded and sharply curved branch from Yelverton to Princetown, England's highest railway station.

(It should be noted that Princetown services always worked with the chimney facing uphill to keep the firebox crown covered; the statement on page 102 [bottom image] of *Western Ways: The Riley Archives Volume 1* that No 4410 is working downhill is incorrect [compiler's error]. The turntable at Princetown was used only for turning snow ploughs.) *Ref PG 391.*

Above: Reading was an important junction where the Berks and Hants line diverged from the Paddington-Bristol route and also where the GWR connected with the Southern Railway. The GWR's establishment was on the upper level, known as Reading General while Southern services to the town terminated at a smaller station on a lower level known as Reading South. From there, the SR route went southwards and eastwards, to points such as Guildford and Redhill to connect with services radiating from London. Passenger services between elsewhere on the GWR and the south-coast were handled at Reading General.

On 19th July 1959, ex-South Eastern & Chatham Railway 4-4-0 Class E1, now BR No 31497, was in store at Reading South shed. This engine was one of ten built in 1920 by Beyer Peacock to an innovative and successful design by Maunsell to overcome weight restrictions on the SECR's Chatham section. This engine left Reading for attention at Nine Elms the same month that this photograph was taken, and returned to service at Salisbury to replace withdrawn 4-4-0s of Class T9. It then moved to Battersea in April 1960 from where it was withdrawn in October that year.

Meanwhile, back on the Western Region 0-6-0 Class 2251 No 2299 is standing at the top of the incline from the Southern Region with a transfer duty (Class J Mineral or Empty wagon train) waiting for the road. *RCR Ref 12901-13999 (1045).*

Opposite top: Looking north at Coombe Junction Signal Box (with the passenger platform just visible to the right) on the line between Looe and the network of freight-only lines that served the quarries and mines in the Caradon area on 31st August 1954. Unfortunately no details of this working are provided but the train, hauled by Class 4575 No 5502, could be either a Liskeard-Caradon goods working or a branch freight from Looe returning to Liskeard. If the latter, the train would have to reverse and proceed back towards the camera, turning left (i.e. eastwards) on to the Liskeard loop to climb virtually a complete circle to gain access to the Cornish main line. However, a freight from Looe would require the locomotive and Toad to exchange ends. There being no brake van behind the locomotive, it may therefore be deduced that this service is destined for the Caradon area.

The lofty Moorswater viaduct to the west of Liskeard that carries the Cornish main line can be seen in the background. *RCR Ref 15000-16250 (945).*

Opposite bottom: On 15th July 1959 Class 5101 No 4150 was passing Newton Abbot East Signal Box with a transfer freight working of 12 open wagons but no brake van. There were a couple of 20-ton wagons in the rake and it is speculated that this might have been the movement of locomotive coal to the depot from Hackney yard, as a trip working within station limits. *RCR Ref 12901-13999 (977).*

Left: Canton-allocated 56xx No 6600 was working a Class K pick-up goods at Newton Abbot on 30th March 1957. Foreigners were sometimes drafted in on loan during the summer to help out with banking duties and sharply increased traffic volumes but a Cardiff engine present in March suggests another reason. The prominent weld line along the tank side indicates that a wasted lower section has recently been cut out and replaced. This feature coupled with the smart condition suggests that the locomotive is most likely not long from overhaul. The tank lining curves around and below the cab side shutters rather than disappearing under them, a styling feature peculiar to Newton Abbot works and not officially sanctioned by Swindon. It is concluded that following a recent local overhaul, No 6600 was on test. However, given human nature, a useful locomotive in first class condition might have been too tempting and on local initiative, it is possible that its "testing" period had been extended until Canton would noisily demand its return. *Ref PG989.*

Bottom: Silverton station was located in open country between Stoke Cannon and Hele & Bradninch (about one mile west of the latter) and over a mile distant from its namesake village. An unusual feature was staggered platforms either side of a secondary road that crossed the railway at this point. The Up platform is out of shot to the right.

Peter Gray's photograph carries the cryptic comment "shunting" but does not elaborate. It seems that on 9th December 1961, small prairie No 5560 has reversed its quite long Class K pick-up goods into the refuge siding. The train seems to comprise empty open wagons except for the pair which have sheeted loads. These have been detached from the train and are apparently being drawn out on the main line, but to what purpose cannot be established. *Ref PG2792.*

Right: From the mid-19th Century with growth in the number of steamships, Kingswear/ Dartmouth became an important participant in the coal trade as the principal port in South Devon for the refuelling of merchant vessels. From 1868, three hulks were moored in the estuary for fuel storage, and up until 1914 the sale of bunker coal was the port's principal trading activity with 750 ships arriving for this purpose in 1890, the peak year. Also, Castle Line (established in 1872) operated its South African service from there until 1891 when it moved its UK port operations to Southampton and Plymouth, before merging with Union Line in 1900.

Kingswear continued to serve as a coaling port, relying on a weekly train comprising 40-ton bogie wagons that brought in bunker fuel from Blaenavon. This was transhipped from the railway by means of the GWR's 360 ft quay that lay parallel with the station platforms. In the return direction, coastal trading vessels called with specialist coal-based fuels that were unloaded by a pair of electric cranes equipped with grab buckets that discharged directly into wagons on the quayside. On 18th July 1958, a remnant of the Kingswear coal trade was found in this train of coke (headcode pick-up or branch goods train) hauled Class 94xx No 8451 (Yorkshire Engine Co Maker's No 2434, built 1949) coming off the Torbay branch at Aller. The load was presumably destined for a gas works somewhere in the west. *RCR Ref 11801-12900 (684).*

Bottom: By 1954, the few "Dukedog" 4-4-0s remaining in Devon were usually employed in piloting passenger services between Newton Abbot and Plymouth. This view dated 16th May 1954 is described as No 9023 departing Newton on a Down fish train running under Class C head code comprising empty vans destined for Churston (for Brixham) and Kingswear. The Dukedogs were the last in a long line of GWR outside-framed 4-4-0s, being a synthesis of Bulldog frames and Duke Class boilers. No 9023 entered service in February 1939 using the frames from unnamed Bulldog No 3423 and the boiler from Duke No 3253 *Boscawen*, and was withdrawn in July 1957. *Ref PG407.*

At times when there were no express passenger or heavy freight services in evidence on a major trunk route the railway could present near bucolic scenes such as this. On a sunny 19th May 1956, 0-6-0PT Class 94xx No 8458 (built by Yorkshire Engine Co Makers No 2441 in May 1950) is ambling along on the Up slow near Tilehurst at the head of a pick-up goods train. Despite the arrival of all-steel open wagons in large numbers, all but two are still timber-bodied. The cargo in the first of these cannot be identified but the fourth, a 5-plank open, carries a container. The remaining six are seven-plankers loaded with coal, and all have seen plenty of service judging by their condition. No 8458 has passed what seems to be another class member running light engine on the Down slow. *RCR Ref 7101-8100 (136).*

The Moretonhampstead branch passenger service was in the hands of large prairie No 4150 on 19th February 1959. The train comprised two non-corridor coaches, an All Third (possibly a bow-ended 56' 8" Diagram C56 or a flat-ended 55' 3" Diagram C66) and a Brake Composite (a B/E Diagram E140 or a F/E Diagram E147). Both the brake composite diagrams were built primarily for use in 2-coach B-sets.

In the interval before returning to Newton Abbot, the prairie has left the passenger coaches at the platform to sort some wagons standing in the goods yard. *Ref PG 1726.*

Hayle is located 1½ miles east of St Erth (junction for the St Ives branch) on the Cornish mainline. From there a branch about one mile long served the wharves on the east bank of the River Hayle estuary. This stub was one of many short freight-only branches that served docks, mines, factories etc, often marked by sharp curves and uneven, overgrown track. On 14th July 1961, pannier tank No 3635 was returning up the branch with a train comprising three tank wagons, a modern 16-ton mineral wagon and a Toad. The first and third tank wagons would appear to be for petroleum products while the second is specifically for transport of sulphuric acid. *Ref PG 2635.*

Above: Even before the arrival of the railway, Helston was an important centre for agriculture as well as tin and copper mining. Connection with the rail network was completed by means of an eight mile branch to Gwinear Road in 1887 and for many years Helston remained busy with goods traffic predominating, except during the holiday season. The branch penetrated difficult country so the line abounded in curves and gradients as steep as 1 in 60. Until dieselisation and the introduction of North British-built Bo Bo Class 63xx, it was the exclusive preserve of small prairie classes 45xx and 4575.

On 24th July 1957, No 4505 was busily engaged in shunting vans at Helston (the most southerly railway station in mainland Britain). The yard is quite crowded with a rail-borne crane and runner rather in the way on the goods shed road while a Toad has apparently been stowed on the run-round loop. A two-coach B-set was the usual formation for branch passenger trains and there appears to be an example standing at the platform.

Helston was famous from 1903 for the pioneer GWR omnibus service that conveyed tourists from there to The Lizard peninsular, England's most southerly point. The Helston branch closed to passengers in November 1962, and two years later to goods. *Ref PG1127.*

Opposite: St Dennis Junction on the Par-Newquay line was an important marshalling point for china clay workings emanating from the goods-only branch network, the main route of which ran in a generally south -easterly direction to connect with the Plymouth-Penzance route at Burngullow. Just south of St Dennis, the 4-mile long Retew Branch diverged southwards from the Burngullow line and terminated at Meledor Mill. On 11th July 1955, pannier tank No 3635 worked the branch and was seen shunting at the terminus. *RCR Ref 6101-7100 (160).*

Chapter 5
China clay

Cornwall is a major producer of china clay (kaolin) which is mined at a number locations but principally in the St Austell district. Transportation of this valuable substance which has a number of industrial applications was a major reason for the establishment of the Cornwall Minerals Railway which was absorbed by the GWR in 1896. China clay was shipped by rail direct to UK consumers, and also to the ports of Fowey and Par for export to foreign buyers, and for delivery by coastal shipping services to UK users.

Originally a variety of railway wagons were used for this traffic but experience led to construction at Swindon in 1913 of a fleet of 500 purpose-designed unfitted vehicles (Diagram O13). The

density of china clay is such that one ton occupies a volume of 28 cubic feet, and it was concluded that wagons of 12 tons capacity were ideal for these services. China clay was largely transported in block trains but rakes of Diagram O13 wagons were also included in ordinary goods services.

Outwardly they resembled standard 5-plank timber Open wagons but with special features to optimise their effectiveness. All were equipped with end-tipping doors as this was the normal means of discharge, plus side doors for clay that might be shipped in barrels. Timber bodies minimised rust contamination of the cargo, and the body planks were of equal width to facilitate repairs. Floor planks were longitudinal to ease end-discharge although zinc-plating was later installed for this purpose, and also to eliminate wet rot of the floors. When loaded, the wagons were covered with canvas sheeting to protect the clay leading to the nickname "hoods". The normal means of canvas protection for Open wagons was in the form of the single hinged longitudinal strut which when erected created the familiar tent-like profile. The end-tipping doors of Diagram O13 prevented use of this method so an arrangement of support struts was installed within each wagon body to prevent the hood from sagging.

Dean-Churchward Type II brakes were favoured as the operating handle on both sides could be located at the non-tipping (i.e. cleaner) end, thus reducing the risk of clogging from residual wet clay. The fleet continued in service until 1959/ 60. Despite their special features, the hoods were a somewhat old-fashioned means of moving a bulk industrial cargo but they were effective in coping with the unusual physical restrictions at Par docks.

China clay trains were worked to the ports by the usual assembly of tank locomotives found in the area (panniers and prairies). However, from 1929 until 1960 there was continuously at least two of 2-8-0T Class 42xx allocated in the west for this traffic. Usually they were shedded at St Blazey although for periods one engine might be switched to Laira, and at busy times another might be drafted in from South Wales to help. Some were long term residents e.g. Nos 4200 (1929-33); 4206 (1952-9); 4215 (1933-43 & 1947-51); 4247 (1952-9); 4298 (1932 & 1934-52); 5274 (1929-32). There were other Class 42xx allocations to English sheds (Gloucester, St Philips Marsh, Swindon, Shrewsbury) but these were for limited periods. The St Blazey allocation was the most enduring with a pattern of duties not dissimilar to those applied on a much wider scale with the South Wales coal traffic.

Left: View from the balcony of the Toad as No 3635 hauls loaded wagons north towards St Dennis junction. *RCR Ref 6101-7100 (162).*

**Opposite top: On 11th July 1955 having returned to St Dennis Junction with its load from the Retew branch, No 3635 has drawn its train on to the Newquay line and then ran round to depart eastwards. Small prairie No 4526 had been added as banking locomotive and the ensemble is now on its way to St Blazey/ Par. On the horizon can be seen several white waste tips that are so characteristic of china clay mining.
*RCR Ref 6101-7100 (171).***

On 8th September 1955, No 3635 was arriving at St Blazey with a Class K Pick Up or Branch goods that combines a rake of loaded hoods with wagons collected from other points. *Ref PG 702.*

Above: St Blazey for long was home to a heterogeneous collection of pannier tanks as exemplified by this view taken of a china clay train approaching Middleway Crossing, Par. As apparent from another photograph taken seconds earlier, this train comprises three cattle wagons and a lengthy rake of empty china clay wagons. Steam unfortunately obscures much of the locomotive but it is No 2182 of Wolverhampton-built Class 2021. This engine was built as saddle tank No 2125 in May 1903, and fitted with pannier tanks in December 1912. It was modified at Swindon in July 1939 with increased brake power and a closed cab, and then renumbered 2182. Ten were so treated and No 2182 was the last survivor of the group being withdrawn in August 1955. The date is 3rd September 1954 and judging by the amount of steam leaking, this veteran was in run down condition although it could still be trusted with a substantial load. The fishtail end to the fixed distant signal arm is worthy of note. *RCR Ref R5001-6100 (383).*

Opposite top: 2-8-0T No 4273 and 0-6-0PT No 9680 on a Down china clay empties train near St Blazey on 18th July 1960. This eight-coupled tank was the last to be drafted in, arriving at St Blazey from Llantrisant in June 1960 and was also the last to stay in Cornwall being moved on to Llanelly in December 1961. It was withdrawn from Barry shed in October 1964. *RCR Ref 14000-15099 (1105).*

Opposite bottom: No 4273 entering Fowey station with a loaded china clay train on 23rd September 1960. An unidentified Class 4575 small prairie stands in the bay with a BR-built auto trailer. *RCR Ref 15100-16250 (273).*

China clay

Above: Later the same day (23rd September 1960) No 4273 has returned to Fowey station from the docks with empties and is waiting while a loaded train, for which the board is off, passes towards the port. *RCR Ref 15100-16250 (274).*

Opposite top: No 4273 is now drawing away from Fowey with its empties, and from this angle it is apparent that the Class 4575 in the bay is at the head of at least three coaches suggesting that although the first was an auto coach, this train was not working in auto mode.

This view presents some mysteries as although the 2-8-0T is clearly on the move, the starting signal remains On. This could not have been to ensure that its train has cleared the loop as in this and the previous picture, the board is Off for the loaded train going in the opposite direction. Further, it is apparent from the following sequence of photographs that Dick Riley joined the footplate at this station as the next two views were taken on that journey.

As so often in Riley photographs, vignettes of the railway scene are also captured – in this case the workmen busy on the awning and roof of the station building. *RCR Ref 15100-16250 (277)* .

Opposite bottom: Approaching Pinnock Tunnel (1173 yards) almost half way along the four miles of route from Fowey station to St. Blazey. *RCR Ref 15100-16250 (281).*

At a stand beyond Pinnock Tunnel. The board states:

ALL DOWN GOODS AND
MINERAL TRAINS MUST
STOP DEAD HERE

Gradients presented particular problems for the operation of non-fitted trains. For successful ascent it was a matter of adequate power for the load while provision of a banking locomotive gave added safety in preventing wagons from running away should the train divide.

For descent, the measures were more complex. It was a usual requirement to limit the speed of unfitted trains to 20 mph and before starting the down grade, the tender brake would be fully screwed down and the guard would do likewise with the Toad brake. Speed was then controlled by application of the locomotive brake as necessary.

This procedure was not possible with a tank engine as the handbrake screwed down concurrent with application of the locomotive brake could result in excessively hot brake shoes.

Thus, for tank engine-hauled trains and for all trains approaching down gradients steeper than 1 in 60, there was a requirement to halt at the Stop Board, which wherever possible was located on a level section of track. The guard would then walk forward and pin down some manual wagon brakes behind the locomotive. The train would then draw forward slowly onto the gradient and the guard would continue to pin down the brakes of passing wagons. Once the driver judged that a sufficient number of wagon brakes had been applied to provide adequate resistance against the weight of the train, he would signal by two sharp whistle blasts that he had sufficient control and that the guard could return to his Toad. During this process both locomotive and Toad brakes would remain off so as to provide a reserve of brake power to keep speed in check on the descent. At the foot of the gradient the train would stop to allow the guard to unpin the wagon handbrakes. These procedures underlined the individual skills required of personnel involved, and of the importance of close working co-operation between locomotive crew and guard.

Descent of gradients by unfitted trains significantly affected elapsed journey times, as demonstrated on Glyn Neath bank (5½ miles at 1 in 47) on the Vale of Neath line. Stop boards were in place at the top and bottom of the bank, and also at the half-way point resulting in an allowance of 42 minutes for the downward passage of a train. Experiments with a train weighing 850 tons showed that the timing could be reduced by 13 minutes if partially fitted, and by 20 minutes if fully fitted. Over undulating routes and with a

maximum speed limit 20 mph, the pinning down procedure could significantly extend elapsed timings, and it was not unusual for a train to average 5-8 mph over a complete journey.

These were standard procedures that could be modified to accommodate local working conditions by means of "footnotes" issued to specific signal boxes, with the approval of the District Inspector. These dispensations would be revised from time-to-time and their application was on the strict condition that the preceding version was immediately destroyed, for obvious reasons. Some issues of these footnotes might still exist but it would be almost impossible now to verify procedures applying to particular locations e.g. it seems probable that special instructions would have been in place concerning descent of gradients such as Dainton, Rattery, and Hemerdon. *RCR Ref 15100-16250 (283).*

Above: The dense network of stub lines and sidings that served the china clay workings abounded in poorly laid, uneven track which necessitated the allocation to St Blazey of Classes 850 and 2021. By the mid-1950s these handy little engines with their modest axle loadings had almost completely disappeared to be replaced by BR-built 0-6-0PT Class 16xx (a pure GWR-based design). Here on the morning of 8th July 1955, No 1626 is leaving St Blazey yard bound for the Goonbarrow branch with eleven china clay empties and a pair of conventional, apparently loaded, 5-plank wagons immediately in front of the Toad. Inserted behind the locomotive is what appeared to be a Macaw (bogie bolster) but its load cannot be discerned.

This is another of Dick Riley's panoramic views that captures so much of the everyday atmosphere of the contemporary railway. *RCR Ref 6101-7100 (89).*

On 6th July 1955, Class 4575 No 5521 was piloting Class 8750 No 3635 on an Up train of loaded hoods approaching Par on the Cornish mainline. *RCR Ref 6101-7100 (65).*

Despite trespass into the world of industrial steam, views of operations at Par Harbour are necessary to complete the china clay story. Access to the docks was by means of a bridge with 8 feet headroom under the Cornish mainline, followed by sharp curves, the tightest of which had a radius of 70 feet.

From 1912 onwards, steam power was provided by diminutive vertical boilered and conventional tank engines that were subjected to modification through local enterprise with varied success. In 1937, W.G. Bagnall supplied a purpose-designed 0-4-0ST (works No 2572) which became *Judy* (one of the earlier engines had been named *Punch)*. With a maximum height of 7' 6", driving

wheels of 2' 9" diameter, 5' 0" wheelbase, and a squat cab with small, narrow footplate set between the frames a little above rail level, the design circumvented the harbour system's demanding physical restrictions. In 1953, Bagnall supplied *Alfred* (Works No 3058) to the same basic design but with some small improvements that made it slightly heavier.

They were the last steam locomotives at work in normal service in Cornwall. *Judy* was retired in 1969 when expensive boiler repairs could not be justified in face of declining use of rail for china clay traffic while *Alfred* worked on until 1977. The pair survive in preservation.

China clay

Top: The Par Harbour shunters on 20th July 1960. The saddle tanks of *Judy* on the left had exposed rivets whereas those for *Alfred* on the right were flush-headed. The closed cab was necessary for safety reasons but the timber shutters at the rear were invariably open, presumably because of the heat generated in the confined space. *RCR Ref 15100-16250 (49).*

Middle: This three-quarter front view of *Judy* dated 20th July 1960 emphasises Bagnall's success with the design. Use of Bagnall-Price valve gear obviated the requirement for a pit for servicing purposes. Ingenuity must have been needed to contain the height of the boiler fittings while the upper edge of the front buffer beam had to be dished to enable opening of the smokebox door. *RCR Ref R15100-16250 (50).*

Bottom: *Judy* (left) and *Alfred* together on the Quay at Par. Their consistently spotless condition contrasted with the clay stained wagons they shunted, and with the perpetual white dust of their working environment. *RCR Ref 5001-6100 (360).*

Chapter 6
Minerals

COAL

The Great Western, which pre-1923 had been Britain's largest railway company measured by route mileage, emerged from the Grouping in buoyant mood. Formation of the other three of the Big Four entailed forced marriages between organisations that had sometimes been committed and not always friendly rivals. Re-organisation and stabilisation of internal relationships was to prove costly, most evident in the case of the London Midland & Scottish Railway where corporate cohesion took around ten years to establish.

The GWR's expansion was mainly concerned with absorption of the Welsh railways. The Old Company's senior administrative structure remained essentially intact while integration was conducted sensitively. Competent personnel encountered little or no diminution in status within the larger body, and construction of 0-6-2T Class 56xx was a sensible acknowledgement of well-established operating practices in the Valleys. Even the sensation of the moment, the new Castle Class, carried names with a heavy bias towards structures found in the Principality.

Grouping of the railways had been an organisational necessity following the Great War which had contributed to erosion of the value of the Welsh inheritance and to long term failure to fulfil the optimistic expectations of the early 1920s. Manpower shortages and sharply increased energy demands during the conflict had dictated extraction from the more accessible coal seams so mining in peacetime became comparatively more expensive. Economic recession later in that decade and other social elements that are well beyond the scope of this work played their part in steady decline of the region's fortunes.

In later years Barry became a steam mecca for all the well-known reasons, but looking around, it was clear that the famous scrapyard was located in an area of industrial dereliction. As poignant as the rusting locomotives were, the massive dockside loading facilities served as abandoned monuments to lost export markets. Nevertheless, during the period covered by this chapter there remained plenty of work for traditional motive power in the Valleys.

Opposite top: On 3rd June 1953, Dick Riley visited the line between Llanelly and Cross Hands in Carmarthenshire. This 13-mile route had been opened as the Llanelly & Mynydd Mawr Railway in 1881 principally to transport coal from Cross Hands and Great Mountain collieries. The system was similar to other Welsh concerns engaged in the movement of coal from pit to port and in the working of miners' trains, but differed in never providing a public passenger service. Now completely closed, it was therefore less well known and seemingly less photographed than the more prominent railways in South Wales.

The LMMR had a difficult start and for a period was operated by the contractor who had built the line. The railway's facilities were basic but following passage of the Light Railways Act 1896, consideration was given to up-grading to permit passenger services. However, the absence of signalling, coupled with uneven trackwork and abundance of sharp curves made the necessary improvements financially prohibitive. Around about 1950 large coal deposits were discovered near Cynheidre, roughly half way along the route and prior to opening of a new colliery in 1960, the lower section was improved to allow use of 2-8-0T Class 42xx and 0-6-2T Class 56xx. The upper section remained the sole preserve of smaller 0-6-0 tank locomotives, as had the rest of the LMMR prior to the improvements.

With axle loading a major constraint, Llanelly shed's allocation in 1934 included eleven members of 0-6-0PT Class 850 (of which three were specifically designated for the LMMR section), and three of Class 2021. Class 850 had been introduced in 1874 so understandably only a pair remained by December 1947 plus ten of Class 2021 (introduced 1897). By the time of Dick Riley's visit, these veterans had given way to lightweight 0-6-0PT Class 16xx, built by British Railways in the small pannier tank tradition. This class seems to have provided the only motive power prior to completion of the improvements mentioned above. Working the line was no sinecure as there were 6 miles with a ruling gradient of 1 in 48 as far as Cynheidre. From there to Cross Hands the line went through undulating country but continued to climb albeit without steep gradients.

Recourse to double-heading uphill was frequently necessary. However, in the tradition of Welsh coal traffic, it was feasible to use modestly powered locomotives as loaded trains worked downhill when the governing factors were speed containment and adequate locomotive/ Toad brake power. This view taken from the balcony of a Toad shows a long train of empty wagons hauled by 0-6-0PT Nos 1607 and 1618 climbing towards Cynheidre. *RCR Ref 3949-4941 (4).*

The same train arriving at Great Mountain Colliery, Tumble. A National Coal Board 0-6-0ST was shunting in the sidings below the slag heaps. *RCR Ref R3949-4941 (6).*

Pannier tank Nos 1607 (left) and 1618 shunting at Great Mountain Colliery sidings. Most of the wagons in view are of the timber-bodied, ex-private owner variety. No 1607 was still resident at Llanelly in 1965 when it was sold to the National Coal Board to work at Cynheidre Colliery thereby achieving the sad distinction of being the last Swindon-built locomotive in commercial service west of Swansea. In 1969, having suffered a cracked frame, it was withdrawn and broken up at the colliery. *RCR Ref 3949-4941 (7).*

Pannier tank and loaded train returning to Llanelly over the LMMR route. *RCR Ref 3949-4941 (15).*

Above: Apart from locomotives (mainly 0-6-2Ts) inherited from the South Wales companies, the Great Western relied principally upon 0-6-2T Class 56xx and 2-8-0T Class 42xx for shifting the vast tonnages extracted from the Valleys. In this undated view, No 5228 trundles westward through Cardiff General at the head of a lengthy Type H unfitted freight train, mainly comprising timber-bodied open wagons. Class 42xx was one of those GWR classes that was built over a long period. Introduced in 1910, by 1930 there were 195 of the type in service but 54 were rebuilt as 2-8-2Ts later that decade. Then, rather unexpectedly, ten more 2-8-0Ts appeared in 1940.

The 2-8-0T wheel arrangement was unique in the UK, although the South Eastern & Chatham Railway came close to building some heavy shunters in 1921, probably at the behest of senior ex-Swindon personnel at Ashford. The 42xx mainly worked heavy, short distance trains which meant that their career mileages were comparatively modest. Operationally they were sure-footed and highly regarded, earning the reputation of never slipping on starting. They survived almost to the end of steam on the Western Region, the class becoming extinct in the Autumn of 1965.

A Castle (another GWR class built over a long period) stands in the far platform – possibly No 5007 *Rougemont Castle*. RCR Ref R3949-4941 (28).

Bottom: No details for this view are recorded in the Archives but the location would seem to be Leckwith junctions, Cardiff. The left hand lamp iron facing the locomotive carries a circular white disc bearing the figures "B 25" which was known as a target, revealing this working as a "control train". Many coal movements were not timetabled but worked by a system administered "on the hoof" by the Control Office. Locomotives and brake vans were made available at specific times daily for use on routes that were then determined by traffic controllers depending on prevailing demand. The target letter indicated the shed from which the locomotive commenced its working day and the number identified the specific duty to which it had been allocated. Target codes and related duties were defined in the Service Time Tables, and the board (either circular or triangular in shape) was carried on the left hand lamp iron (facing the locomotive). An ordinary lamp was carried on the right hand iron.

This locomotive has started its day from Barry shed (B =). Other target prefixes were:- C = Cardiff Cathays; D = Cardiff East Dock; F = Ferndale; H = Cardiff Canton; J = Abercynon; K = Dowlais (Caeharris); M = Merthyr; PR = Pontypool Road; R = Rhymney; T = Treherbert; X = Coke Ovens; Y = Radyr. The target carried by 0-6-2T No 5609 suggests that a train of empty coal wagons has been collected at the docks and worked up the ex-Barry Railway line, turning westwards at Leckwith junctions and is about to join the ex-GWR mainline before branching off northwards to enter one of the Valleys. *RCR Ref 2199 to 3948 (48).*

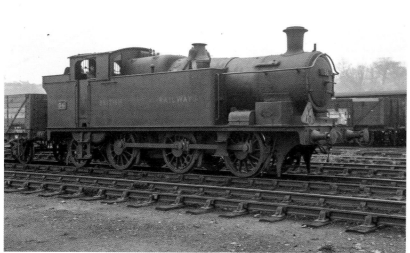

Seen here in Radyr yard on 5th May 1951, 0-6-2T No 56 had started life in May 1910 as Rhymney Railway No 14, built by Robert Stephenson & Co (Maker's No 3391). It was fitted with a Standard No 10 boiler in April 1936 and must have been repainted since nationalisation as its side tank carry the legend "BRITISH RAILWAYS" in economy plain font. The triangular target board seems to have been favoured by Radyr depot. This locomotive was withdrawn in September 1953. *RCR Ref 2199-3948 (377).*

The GWR's numerically largest class was the ubiquitous 57xx/ 8750 family, examples of which reached virtually every corner of the network. Less widely travelled were Nos 6700 to 6749 built 1930/ 1 by W.G. Bagnall and Yorkshire Engine Co (25 locomotives each) as part of a government scheme to relieve unemployment. Nos 6750 to 6779 were built at Swindon between 1946 and 1950 with the more modern 8750-style cab. Both versions of the 67 series were fitted with steam brakes only plus three-link couplings, thus restricting them to wagon shunting and unfitted haulage. Nos 6700-09 spent their entire careers at Cardiff East Dock shed where No 6706 (built April 1930 by W.G. Bagnall, Maker's No 2388) was photographed on 5th August 1951. *RCR Ref 2199 to 3948 (667).*

This is Penrhos Junction, a location that illustrates the complex nature of the Welsh Valleys network. The four track "mainline" is actually two pre-Grouping routes in parallel. The pair of lines on the left were the Taff Vale Railway's Walnut Tree Branch that about a mile to the west curved away southwards to join the TVR mainline at Taff's Well. The pair of tracks to the right from Penrhos onwards were the property of the Alexander (Newport & South Wales) Docks & Railway (ADR) which ran from this point in a westerly direction for about half a mile before turning northward to connect with the TVR at Pontypridd.

The bridge piers just visible in the background, originally carried the rails of the Barry Railway's route (known as the Penrhos branch) that crossed over, but made no physical connection with, the TVR and ADR lines. The BR line was opened in 1901 from Tynycaeau Junction near St Fagans and continued northwards up the Rhymney Valley, completely avoiding the Caerphilly yards and complex to the east, to connect with the Brecon & Merthyr Railway (BMR) at Duffryn Isaf (formerly Barry Junction), between Bedwas and Llanbradach. The Penrhos branch formed part of grandiose plans by the BR in conjunction with the BMR to complete a competing route between Barry and Newport that never came to fruition. This venture in part had stemmed from the Rhymney Railway's refusal to grant running powers to the BR over its network.

Post-Grouping, the GWR retained the BR's St Fagans-Penrhos segment but recognised that the northern section of the Penrhos branch was an unnecessary duplication. It was therefore closed completely in 1926 and the spans of the overbridge were removed, once a new connecting line had been installed so that traffic from Barry/ St Fagans joined the TVR line at Penrhos Junction.

Class 72xx No 7240 on a Cardiff Cathays control train (target C16) has come up the Walnut Tree Branch having turned off the TVR main line at Taffs Well and was passing Penrhos Junction Signal Box on 12th May 1952 with a long string empty wagons bound for the Rhymney Valley. The exhaust of the banking locomotive is just visible in the distance. Meanwhile, on the extreme left, a southbound loaded train has diverged onto the connecting line at the start of the remaining segment of the ex-BR Penrhos branch, presumably destined for Barry docks. *RCR Ref 2199 to 3948 (773)*.

Above: Penrhos Junction looking eastward. The connecting line from the remaining section of the BR Penrhos branch joined the TVR Walnut Tree branch immediately in front of the signal box. Beyond the road overbridge can just be distinguished the second junction where the ADR and TVR routes combine at Walnut Tree Branch Junction into two tracks before splitting almost immediately at Beddau Branch Junction. At that point, the left-hand route turns northwards towards Caerphilly yards and then up the Rhymney valley while the right-hand route leads to Caerphilly station.

The train of empty wagons must be approaching under caution as an auto train comprising a matchboard trailer propelled by a Class 54xx or 64xx pannier tank has just cleared Beddau Branch Junction, bound for Pontypridd. *RCR Ref 2199 to 3948 (779).*

Opposite top: Returning for more on 12th May 1952. A reasonably clean Class 56xx No 5653 was passing Penrhos Junction with an Up train of empties consisting of timber-bodied vehicles so typical of that period. The second behind the locomotive appears to be numbered P96369 but its previous private owner identity is evident in the wording "CITY OF BIRMINGHAM ELECTRIC DEPARTMENT". A photograph taken seconds earlier of this train approaching shows no target indicating that this was probably a timetabled service. It was normal practice for Class 56xx working in the valleys to face uphill i.e. loaded downhill trains always ran with the trailing truck leading. *RCR Ref 2199 to 3948 (778).*

Opposite bottom: Ex-Taff Vale Railway 0-6-2T Class A No 405 (built October 1920 by Hawthorn Leslie, Maker's No. 3406, and renumbered by the GWR in 1923 as 391) at Radyr Yard on 5th May 1951. A "C15" target board is hung on the left hand lamp iron (facing the locomotive).

Class A was the Taff Vale's numerically largest class. Equipped with 5' 3" driving wheels they were originally intended as mixed traffic machines but spent their later careers mainly on coal haulage. This engine was rebuilt with a Swindon Standard No 10 boiler in October 1928, and received larger cylinders with increased boiler pressure in June 1933. It was withdrawn in June 1953. *RCR Ref 2199 to 3948 (371).*

Ex-Rhymney Railway 0-6-2T Class A No 117 (renumbered by the GWR in 1923 as 73) was at Radyr Yard on 5th May 1951 carrying the rather unlikely Class A Express Passenger head code. Built by Robert Stephenson & Company (Maker's No 3394) in July 1910, this locomotive was one of five to retain its original boiler whereas the majority received the Swindon Standard No 10, a favourite in the "westernisation" process of South Wales tank engines. This locomotive, in virtually original condition except for the GWR safety valve bonnet, was withdrawn in July 1952. *RCR Ref 2199 to 3948 (372).*

Enshrined within a seminal legal decision dating back to the mid-19th Century, before World War 2 a major proportion of coal was still moved in wagons owned by collieries and merchants. At its height, the private owner fleet exceeded 600,000 vehicles and its operation was chronically inefficient. Shortcomings had been long recognised and redress of a fundamentally unsound system commenced during World War 1 through the common pooling of wagons owned by railway companies. Efforts to encourage the inclusion of wagons owned by merchant and collieries in the pool met with almost no success but this parlous situation was rectified by nationwide requisition on the outbreak of World War 2. Standardisation of ex-PO wagon numbers under the P-prefixed system was attempted by British Railways but abandoned in 1957. On 26th July 1952, this loaded coal train at Leckwith, Cardiff consists mainly of ex-PO vehicles but three are the more efficient 20-ton variety of GWR origin. The first and third would seem to be end-tipping (both ends) wagons of Diagram N28 or N29 of *circa* 1935, fitted with Morton brakes. Livery variety is evident with one labelled "LOCO" while the other carries diagonal white lines to indicate that both ends have tipping doors. The middle wagon is of an older vintage with rounded corners, possibly diagram N2 of 1906.

The most distinctive feature of this train was the motive power in the form of 4-6-0 Saint Class No 2906 *Lady of Lynn*, looking very much out of place on this humble Class J mineral working. Built in May 1906, this Cardiff Canton-based engine, a late survivor of an illustrious class, was withdrawn the following August. The BR-style smokebox number plate looked out of place on these veterans but the tender still proudly carries the initials G W R. The Saints as a class became extinct in 1953 and were much missed – at least until the re-incarnation of 2019. *RCR Ref 2199 to 3948 (1012).*

The sea wall between Sprey Point and where the line turned inland towards Teignmouth station was one of Dick Riley's favourite locations. A non-fitted Down Class H freight with all the open wagons in view loaded with what appears to be locomotive coal was approaching with Class 28xx No 2803 in charge on 19th July 1956. The railway was a significant customer for its own needs and preferred the use of 4-wheel and bogie wagons of 20 and 40 tons capacity respectively. Operating economics strongly favoured higher capacity vehicles but in GWR days, many of the South Wales collieries did not have suitable loading facilities. As a result, the efforts of Felix Pole (General Manager) to hire out to the collieries 20-ton all steel wagons built at Swindon (known as Pole wagons) met with only limited success. A number of the wagons in this train are of 20 ton capacity.

The cost of moving locomotive coal from South Wales to depots in the South West was one reason behind the GWR's 1939 evaluation of route electrification beyond Taunton. While that proposal did not proceed, the fuel supply problem remained which is why services to Devon and Cornwall were among the first to be dieselised by BR Western Region. *RCR Ref 7101-8100 (663).*

IRONSTONE

Minerals traffic in substantial volumes derived from the ironstone quarries of Oxfordshire which stretched eastwards into the adjacent counties of Warwick and Northants. Ironstone was shipped out by privately-owned quarry railway systems, mainly standard gauge except for some narrow gauge lines as at Hook Norton. During BR days, ironstone was either loaded into Tippler and hopper wagons at the quarries or at transhipment points adjacent to mainline routes.

It was the task of the GWR to move ironstone to industrial consumers in the Midlands and the North of England, and to South Wales. The northbound traffic was worked Down the London-Birmingham main line by way of Leamington Spa and Hatton, and most photographic attention was focussed on the climb of Hatton bank.

Traditionally, some trains for South Wales set out in the Up direction as far as King's Sutton where they branched off to the west onto the Banbury and Cheltenham Railway, a rural route with lengthy single track sections. Unfortunately, there are no images in the Collection of workings over this rather obscure line by way of Bourton-on-the-Water, the flyover crossing the Oxford-Worcester mainline at Kingham, Andoversford Junction (northern extremity of the Midland & South Western junction Railway), and Leckhampton. Trains then turned south over the Hatherley loop to gain the Cheltenham-Gloucester line, and finally down the old South Wales mainline to the west of the River Severn.

Opposite: Hatton Bank on 22nd October 1954. Class 30xx (ROD) No 3028 was putting in a spirited performance with this Down train of about 16 loaded hoppers. Derived from Great Central Railway Class 8K, these sturdily built and highly regarded 2-8-0s were produced in considerable numbers for military service in France in 1917-9, and they later strayed far and wide in Britain and overseas. This particular locomotive was built by Nasmyth Wilson (Maker's No 1281) in early 1919 for military service as ROD No 1725, but never made it to France. It was lent to the Great Central Railway from October that year until August 1921 and was then stored at Royds Green, Leeds until purchased by the GWR in May 1925. It then underwent "Westernisation" (the fitting of various GW components) and worked on unfitted heavy freight haulage until withdrawal in August 1956. *RCR Ref 5001-6100 (585).*

This page: The product of another war, BR WD 2-8-0 No 90572 also tackled Hatton bank on 16th April 1956 in this case with at least 25 hopper wagons exhibiting a variety of profiles and sizes.

The War Department 2-8-0 was a derivation of LMS Stanier Class 8F. Designed by RA Riddles, with extensive use of fabricated and welded parts it was possible to build roughly two WD 2-8-0s in the time required for a single 8F. Between January 1943 and January 1945, North British Locomotive Co completed 545 of the type while Vulcan Foundry delivered 390 between May 1943 and May 1945, a remarkable achievement. BR No 90572 (Maker's No 4931) was part of a batch of 50 built by Vulcan between October and December 1943, initially carrying WD No 7115, changed to 77115 in late 1944. It was on loan to the LNER from new until November 1944 when it was shipped across the Channel and allocated to Aalst, Belgium. Following return (date unknown) to the UK, it was lent to the GWR from May 1947. Part of a batch of 533 purchased in December 1948 by British Railways, it remained allocated to the Western Region (Chester shed as at August 1950) and was withdrawn in February 1966. *RCR Ref 6101-7100 (777).*

Left: This train consisted of over 25 loaded Tippler wagons and is one of the heavier ironstone trains portrayed in this chapter. It is in the hands of Class 28xx No 2812 and has banking assistance as it storms up the Hatton bank relief line. *RCR Ref 6101-7100 (804).*

Bottom: No 6331 enters Leamington Spa on 18th April 1956, with at least 18 loaded hoppers in view – a significant load for a medium-sized mogul. *RCR Ref 6101-7100 (830).*

Opposite top: 19th April 1956, Class 2884 No 3842 cantered through Leamington Spa with another train of laden iron ore tipplers. Class 5101 No 5194 awaits release from the bay platform line. *RCR Ref 6101-7100 (860).*

Below: On 16th April 1956, Class 28xx No 2859 was leading a Down train bound for South Wales comprised entirely of loaded Tippler wagons, a variant on the BR standard 16-ton mineral wagon, near Bearley between Hatton and Stratford-upon-Avon. By this time the Banbury-Cheltenham line was no longer used for South Wales-bound ironstone trains. The route was in process of being rundown and removal of the Hatherley loop at Cheltenham in 1956 necessitated a longer, more circuitous journey. No 2859 would have started northwards Down the Paddington-Birmingham mainline as far as Hatton, then turning southwards at the triangle on to the Bearley Junction – Stratford-on-Avon – Honeybourne – Cheltenham Malvern Road route, and thus on to Gloucester and down the west bank of the Severn.

No 2859 has about 30 wagons in tow making the estimated weight of this train 650 to 700 tons. *RCR Ref 6101-7100 (774).*

This load of ironstone comprising at least 18 Tippler wagons destined for South Wales was approaching Wilmcote between Bearley Junction and Stratford-on-Avon, also on 16th April 1956. Once again, a Class 28xx is in charge and in this case, the locomotive has especial interest in being No 2805 of the first production batch, built October 1905. This locomotive was superheated in October 1910 and fitted with a fully coned boiler in March 1916, but is otherwise in "as built" condition with original square front drop end and inside steam pipes. It is coupled to a rare "intermediate" 3500-gallon tender. Withdrawn in May 1960, No 2805 was one of only four to remain in unmodernised form. The last survivor of this quartet was No 2818 and its original condition was the reason for its inclusion in the National Collection. *RCR Ref 6101-7100.*

No 6907 *Davenham Hall* was on a reverse Up working in Harbury cutting on 18th April 1956, returning with a lengthy rake of empty ironstone hoppers. *RCR Ref 6101-7100 (839).*

Chapter 7
Bankers and Pilots

Brunel's engineering of the South Devon Railway's mainline west of Newton Abbot required scaling the southern shoulder of Dartmoor by means of a curvaceous route that included two summits at Dainton (217 feet above sea level) and then at Wrangaton (666 feet). His intended solution to these barriers was atmospheric traction which promised movement of greater loads at higher speeds than contemporary locomotives could manage, and where adverse gradients would do little to impede progress. That was the theory but before the "Atmospheric caper" had reached that far west, environmental factors led to the system's failure, leaving the gradients in place and a lasting challenge for operating authorities.

Where loads exceeded prescribed limits, fitted trains (passenger, parcels and milk) worked double-headed between Newton Abbot and Plymouth in both directions. Freights trains were given rear-end assistance with the banker dropping off at the conclusion of each climb and returning light engine for the next bout of high energy labour.

These workings attracted much attention from photographers and for good reason. The aggregate nominal tractive effort deployed could be considerable in relation to the train's length. Unusual locomotive pairings appeared at times of motive power shortages. The combination of full forward gear and wide open regulator ensured sight and sound that was deeply evocative of the drama of steam power hard at work.

On 8th June 1955, Prairie No 5113 was piloting Class 2884 No 3843 over the quadruple track section between Aller Junction and Newton Abbot with the 12.20 pm Penzance-Kensington milk train (Class C Fitted). With twelve full 6-wheel milk tankers, a passenger brake van and two Cordons on the rear, this train would have had an aggregate weight of around 400 tons. *Ref PG 681.*

Opposite top: Plymouth-bound pilot engine No 5195 and 2-8-0 No 3864 on 28th July 1957 are approaching Aller Junction, west of Newton Abbot. Described as a (Class C fitted) parcels train, the nature of vehicles in tow suggests that the actual cargo was rather more varied. The first two are modern fish vans followed by a pair of ordinary vans, and then an ex-GWR Passenger Brake Van (probably a bow ender). Then follows three ex-SR utility vans and what seems to be a pair of ex-LNER bogie vans. The remainder of the train is a continued mixture, including what looks like ex-GWR coach. It is this sort of diversity that generates nostalgic memories of services so remote from the blandness of today's block freight and fixed formation passenger trains. *Ref PG 1137.*

Opposite bottom: The Plymouth and Torbay routes parted company at Aller Junction and it was common practice to stow a goods train in the loop at the bottom of Dainton Bank, to await an available path. The location was hardly ideal as it necessitated a standing start immediately before a 1 in 98 gradient that progressively steepens to 1 in 36 over the following two miles. However, the location helped in clearing the often crowded Newton Abbot station environment, and in reducing conflicting traffic movements across the Torquay line.

On 12th March 1955, the board has come off and 2-6-0 Class 43xx No 5321 has set out on the climb with a Class H unfitted load of coal, with plenty of effort from the unidentified banker. The train engine was one of eleven despatched brand new from Swindon to serve with the Railway Operation Division in France between September 1917 and May 1919.

By 1955, the standard BR 16 ton all-steel mineral wagon was present in significant numbers but this train still shows variety in its composition. Immediately behind the tender is a 10-ton ex-GWR Loco coal wagon, and the next two seem to be ex-private owner, the first having been repainted while the second still shows vestiges of its pre-war livery. Two standard BR 16-ton mineral wagons are next but more of the ex-PO variety follow. The brake van seems to be of non-GWR origin. *Ref PG 502A.*

Below: On 25th November 1950, Class 5101 No 5153 is about to join the main Down line from the Aller Loop while rendering vigorous assistance to 2-8-0 Class 47xx No 4701, the head-end power. *Ref PG 101.*

Bankers and Pilots

Opposite top: Serving the purpose for which Aller Loop was installed, on 24th July 1955 Hall Class No 4971 *Stanway Hall* stands at the head of a Class H unfitted freight, banked by Class 61xx No 6107. Passing through is a Class C fitted vans train, described by Peter Gray as a (presumably empty) Fish in the hands of No 4988 *Bulwell Hall* with Class 2251 No 2262 coupled inside. It was official practice with double-headed services for the pilot to follow the train engine but the necessary marshalling during busy periods often prevented application of this discipline.

Although not in view, the presence of a Class 61xx working as banker calls for comment. The date was well before the introduction of diesel multiple units on London suburban services and this class was then fully engaged on those duties. Being mid-summer, motive power was in great demand in the west and it is speculated that the locomotive was on temporary loan to the area from Old Oak Common. *Ref PG 652*.

Opposite bottom: Class 5101 No 4174 and Castle Class No 5028 *Llantilio Castle* storm past the Aller loop in a vigorous assault on Dainton East on 16th June 1959. This complete Class C fitted train is in view and its make-up again reveals the interest provided by the "parcels" category. Of the total of seventeen vehicles, eight were 4-wheel fitted vans. The leading bogie vehicle is a GWR Hawksworth Passenger Brake Van (Diagram K45 or K46); there appear to be four more PBVs, all BR Mark 1s; a single SR Utility van; apparently an LMS Passenger Full Brake and an LNER van; the final vehicle seems to be a GWR-type PBV in blood-and-custard livery. *Ref PG 1880*.

Below: Conventionally, the train locomotive would be larger than the banker but on 28th July 1957 near Stoneycombe Quarry, this service was in the hands of Class 43xx No 6301 while Class 78xx No 7812 *Erlestoke Manor* provided banking help. Manors were often used at this time to assist trains over the south Devon banks but more normally in the role of pilots for passenger, parcel and milk services. *Ref PG 1136*.

Dainton East bank was a favourite location for Peter Gray, probably encouraged by the beautiful local scenery. This Class H unfitted freight, headed by Class 43xx No 6374 and banked by Class 5101 No 4133 has cleared Stoneycombe Gorge on 2nd May 1955. At this point Dainton Tunnel, which marked the end of the climb, would be in sight from the mogul's footplate. *Ref PG 269.*

Class 5101 No 4179 hard at work banking a freight train up Dainton East on 23rd April 1955. A pair of scruffy timber-bodied wagons precede 20 ton Toad No W68824 of Diagram AA20, a type built in considerable numbers between 1934 and 1943. It was preferred practice for the veranda end to lead as this afforded the guard a good view of the train. The other way around, he only had a panoramic view of where the train had been.

Perhaps this is heresy but the familiar Toad, so characteristic of the GWR did not seem a very efficient design. With veranda trailing, the guard only had a forward view through the end windows, which could be poor due to accumulated grime, or by leaning over the balcony side which could make precise control of the brake difficult. British Railways apparently was unimpressed with the concept as GWR Toads were never admitted to the wagon pool. By this stage, brake vans had to be equipped with side duckets but a dispensation was granted to the ex-GWR fleet. They were confined to the Western Region only, hence the "Not in common use" sign emblazoned on the side. *Ref PG 536*

On 19th May 1956, smartly turned out Laira-based Prairie No 5175, with help from sister No 5153 was making good progress, nearing Dainton tunnel with a Class E partially fitted freight (at least four wagons piped to train locomotive). As a general freight service comprising a mixture of vehicles this was a train type that has long since disappeared. The first wagon is a six-wheel Rotank intended to convey two-axle road trailers, usually containing milk. However, the load in this case seems to be a pair of smaller single axle road tanker trailers. Immediately behind there is a shock wagon presumably to help insulate this load from the rest of the train, most of which is probably unfitted *Ref PG 805.*

Dick Riley was adept at producing panoramic views that embraced a wealth of detail as in this portrait of Totnes station. Class 28xx No 2843 has arrived on 15th July 1958 with a Class H unfitted freight service on the Down through road. Boiler pressure is well up with steam feathering from the safety valve so either good progress was made in restoring the fire while coasting down Dainton West bank, or the train has stood time in the Down loop on the eastern bank of the River Dart. At the far end of the Down platform loop stands a large prairie, waiting to reverse out on to the Down main road and buffer up to the Toad.

The railway formed an integral part of the local community in those days. A direct link with Brunel is the pumping house built for the atmospheric system which never reached that far west. This was later incorporated into the creamery complex in the left background and the pumping house can just be discerned as the taller building behind the lorry loading bay. The creamery's production was despatched daily to London by 6-wheel tanker wagons. The sidings on the left contain open wagons, a three plank carrying a container and a solitary milk tanker. The presence of the two suburban brake coaches cannot be readily explained as the Ashburton branch services that terminated at Totnes were formed of Auto coaches.

Behind the banker can be seen the goods shed with evidence of plenty of custom judging by the number of wagons in the immediate vicinity. Behind the shed can be glimpsed the start of the Totnes Quay branch that a few years later would play an important role in the fledgling Great Western Society preservation movement. In April 1962, the Down station building suffered a disastrous fire and was replaced with makeshift buildings from the portacabin architectural design school. Three cattle wagons stand in the Down bay. On the adjacent siding there is a shabby Toplight Brake Third (Diagrams D45, D46, D68 are possibilities) and the chimney in the roof indicates that this 1908-10 vintage vehicle is eking out its career in departmental service. On the same line, a 6-wheel milk tanker awaits transfer across to the creamery sidings. These vehicles were invariably grimy, placing them at odds with the milk industry's endeavours to promote the clean, healthy image of its products. In the foreground there is a typical water crane with its attendant fire devil. *RCR Ref 11801-12900 (607).*

The banker having buffered up at the rear, No 2843 is under way and has commenced the assault on Rattery bank. The train includes five timber-bodied wagons for general merchandise at the front, two empty, two sheeted and one loaded with what appears to be oil drums. The remainder comprises mostly, if not entirely, 16 ton steel-bodied mineral wagons loaded with coal. There appeared to be 20-25 of these suggesting an aggregate weight of around 500 tons.

This was a time when in the absence of trains to admire, the railway offered much else to study. The sidings on the left contain what seems to be a permanent way van at the buffer stops with a Toad behind and a Macaw a little further back. On the adjacent siding stand three open wagons loaded with containers. There is a small merchant's yard to the right where more wagons are standing. The Up approach signal gantry, off-set to the right for sighting purposes on the left hand bend, is located behind the platelayer's hut and the board is off indicating that a train on the Up through road is due.

Despite the steeply graded climb in both directions to the summit at Dainton Tunnel, Rattery was generally considered the most difficult of the four south Devon inclines. The climb starts at 1 in 66 just this side of the road bridge and continues at this sort of gradient, with a couple of short easier sections for the next five miles to Marley tunnel (c.f. Aller Junction to Dainton Tunnel which is a little more than two miles). From Marley the gradient is easier over the next 3½ miles through Brent to the summit at Wrangaton. Thereafter, a tired crew on a through service from London could use the run down Hemerdon to Plymouth to finish off the remains of the cold tea and have a wash using the pep pipe. *RCR Ref 11801-12900 (606).*

Opposite top: Many regarded the 28s as Britain's finest heavy freight design until the arrival of 2-10-0 BR Class 9F in 1954 and this belief is borne out by No 2843, a few yards further into the Rattery climb. Steam is still feathering from the safety valves. The fireman looks relaxed, and happy to have his photograph taken. The overall impression is of a fine locomotive and a competent crew firmly in charge of the allotted task. *RCR Ref 11801-12900 (608).*

Opposite bottom: And here comes No 2843's banker which is now revealed as Class 5101 No 5164. Swindon was then actively applying lined green livery to locomotives beyond the 4-6-0 fleet on the notional basis that they would be employed on passenger services, obviously not the case here. The prairie looks very smart with lining that it never carried in GWR days. The "cycling lion" emblem looks a little out of place as this glorious Indian summer turnout was more usually associated with the "ferret and dartboard". *RCR Ref 11801-12900 (609).*

This page, top: The 2843/ 5164 cavalcade blasts away up Rattery into the distance. *RCR Ref 11801-12900 (610).*

This page, middle: The logistics behind this final chapter in the Rattery saga of Nos 2843 and 5164 are intriguing. The location is described as "near Brent", a station approximately seven miles to the west of Totnes by rail, and rather longer by road. The train had a head start over Dick Riley who would have had to recover his trusty Morris Minor, drive to the Brent area, park the car and set up his photographic location which seems impossible in the time available. It must be concluded that the train had been side-lined in the loop to the east of Brent before reaching this location. *RCR Ref 11801-12900 (611).*

This page, bottom: During the 19th Century, it was common for 0-6-0STs to be used on main line freight haulage, the long-lived and sturdy double-framed "Buffalo" class being a particular favourite for such work. On 7th April 1958, history was repeated with 0-6-0PT Class 57xx No 3629 looking comfortable with a rake of around 22 wagons on a Class H unfitted working near Stoneycombe, but Class 5101 No 5154 was providing substantial rear end assistance. *Ref PG 1391.*

Left: Summer 1958 and this engine must be on loan from elsewhere as it leaves the loop at the foot of Dainton East. The 0-6-2T Class 56xx was invariably associated with coal and commuter traffic in the Welsh valleys although there was always a small contingent in the London division. Accordingly, the appearance of Armstrong Whitworth-built No 6670 in the West Country was noteworthy, the more so as this example has received the then fashionable lined green livery. The train engine was reported as 2-8-0 Class 2884 No 2899. *Ref PG 1795.*

Right: Most photographs of unfitted services on the south Devon inclines show loaded Down trains. Presumably there were fewer convenient sites for photographers on Dainton West and Hemerdon. Also, as most Up mixed freight services were likely to be less than fully loaded, there were fewer opportunities to witness spectacular performances. However, here is a laden Up train in the form of a permanent way working of ballast hoppers. Class 45xx No 4524 is climbing Hemerdon on 31st July 1955, helped by 2-6-2T Class 3150 No 3186.

The Class C head code covered a wide range of fully fitted trains (parcels, fish, fruit, livestock, other perishable cargoes) conforming to coaching stock requirements, and also express freight, livestock, perishable or ballast trains, pipe fitted throughout with automatic vacuum brake operative on not less than half the vehicles. No 4564's train appears to comprise seven ballast hopper wagons plus brake van and could be fitted throughout. The distance makes specific identification impossible but the ballast hoppers appear to be of Diagram P7, a type introduced in 1893 and eventually totalling over 400 examples. In the early 1900s, their capacity was increased by vertical side extensions and a little later, many acquired vacuum and Dean-Churchward brakes. Installation of automatic brakes on a wagon type whose duties were essential yet humble might seem a luxury. However, the measure was necessary as they could be called upon in emergency situations where they were needed to work in express freight mode. *RCR Ref 5001-6100 (859).*

The 41 members of Class 3150 appeared in 1906-8 as the Standard No 4 boilered version of the large prairies. They were often employed as bankers, being particularly associated with Severn Tunnel Junction depot. This group of photographs show No 3186 on such duties in connection with an Up van train on Hemerdon bank on 5th July 1955. Two show the prairie hard at work behind 20-ton Toad No W114930 (of the first

batch of Diagram AA19 built 1927-31) and in the third, it is coasting back down the bank after completion of its allotted task. No 3186 was built in January 1908 and received outside steam pipes in June 1942 while retaining its original square drops ends. It later acquired the curved style as shown here. No 3186 worked on until June 1957 – not a bad innings of over 49 years' hard work. *RCR Refs 6101-7100 (9)/ (10)/ (12).*

Chapter 8
Loose ends

The 21st Century railway is a technocratic marvel that through adoption of modern engineering techniques and sophisticated electronics has achieved extraordinary progress measured in average start-to-stop speeds, operational intensity, and working reliability. These successes are all the more remarkable as excluding the Channel Tunnel services plus Cross Rail and HS2, they use a basic railway network that dates from the mid-19th Century. Elsewhere in countries such as France and Japan high speed progress has relied on brand new railways in their totality. In contrast, Britain offers modernity through fixed formation passenger services, block freight trains, simplified track layouts and bus stop-style architecture in environments that hitherto played host to a transport system of idiosyncratic individuality.

For today's older enthusiast, memories of that heritage focus heavily on the 1950s and awaken recollections of diverse curiosities in train composition and operating practices, some of which appear below.

This was described by Dick Riley as a Down Fish empties. No 7036 *Taunton Castle* was running under Express Goods headcode near Hinksey South Signal Box on 15th August 1959. The spotless condition of the locomotive (the penultimate class member built August 1950) and the train's composition suggests that this might actually be a running-in turn. *RCR Ref 14000-15099 (129).*

Somewhat off-subject for a book about non-passenger services, the operating authorities at St. Blazey would have appreciated the extra "grunt" provided by their small contingent of 2-8-0T Class 42xx. In the tradition of employing unusual motive power at busy times, No 4247 has been relieved of china clay haulage to act as train engine for an empty stock working to Newquay, led by 2-6-2T Class 5101 No 4167. They were starting from Par on Thursday, 2nd September 1954.

The Express Goods head lamp code also covers "Empty stock going to work additional Ordinary, Excursion or Passenger trains", obviously appropriate for this working. The train includes a Brake Composite, an All Third (possibly Diagram C67) plus two "Sunshine" coaches and then what might be a Diagram C54 All Third. The other two coaches in view are too distant for even an approximate indication of their types. The varied composition of the train was typical of many passenger services in the 1950s, especially in the scratch assembly of seasonal "extras". *RCR Ref 5001-6100 (371).*

William Stanier's 2-8-0 Class 8F was the most numerous type introduced during his tenure at the LMS, and he apparently regarded the design as a natural evolution of Churchward's 2-8-0 Class 28xx. Eventually the 8Fs totalled 852 following extensive construction during World War 2 for use in the UK, and for overseas service with the War Department. This programme engaged commercial manufacturers and railway company workshops on a major scale.

The Great Western received 25 of Class 8F on short term loan in 1940/ 1 and then built 80 numbered 8400-79 between 1943 and 1945.

These locomotives were officially LMS property on loan to the GWR; a number stayed on with BR Western Region. Their construction engendered the first major design rethink at Swindon since Churchward's time and CME Hawksworth initiated investigation of several new design options employing features that derived from Stanier's creation. In the GWR's post war construction programme, both the 4-6-0 Counties and the Modified Halls had features that can be traced back to the 8Fs.

No 48436 was built at Swindon in April 1944 and was transferred, on paper at least, to the LMS three years later. It was one that continued to work on BR Western Region and is seen here on a Class H Down unfitted freight approaching Teignmouth on 16th July 1958. The Swindon-built 8Fs were distinguishable by the modified ejector pipe assembly on the left-hand side of the boiler and smokebox.

The arrival of the new order is evident with 0-6-0 diesel shunter (later designated Class 08) No D3521 coupled immediately behind the tender, on delivery to its first depot. *RCR Ref 11801-11800 (631).*

Another of Swindon's 8Fs hard at work on GWR territory, in this case at Birmingham Snow Hill on 24th March 1960. No 48402 was on an Up Class K pick-up goods of around 20 open wagons and those in view seem to be loaded with scrap metal. Stanier never wavered in his allegiance to the GWR and it must have been a source of satisfaction to the finest Chief Mechanical Engineer that the Old Company never had to see this highly-regarded design gainfully employed on "home turf".

WR suburban services had yet to be dieselised judging by the rake in the background. Those in view are apparently a BR Mark 1 All Third, a Hawksworth Diagram D132 Brake Third and a bow ended All Third of Composite of early 1930s vintage.
RCR Ref 14000-15099 (580).

During the summer months of the 1950s and early 1960s, delivery of additional coaching stock to the West Country to cope with the Saturday exodus of returning holidaymakers was a complex logistical exercise. Wherever possible, the extra services were provided with catering facilities and to this end, a train of heterogeneous vehicles departed London for Devon and Cornwall at mid-day on Fridays. On departure they were fully provisioned and staffed (the latter slept overnight in their vehicles). A lengthy stop was made at Exeter to re-charge gas tanks and the train was split at Newton Abbot, some coaches going down the Torbay branch and the remainder continuing to Newquay and Penzance.

In this view at Torre on 10th May 1958, the return working of a Cafeteria Car has been arranged by its addition to an auto train as far as Newton Abbot. The summer timetable did not commence until Monday, 9th June that year so this vehicle must have been in Devon for some other purpose. Nevertheless, it was typical of the sort of catering coach that would be drafted in to help with heavy summer weekend traffic demands.

The revenue-earning element of this working is a conventional combination of 0-4-2T No 1427 and a pair of 1951-vintage auto trailers of 63' Diagram A38. They were built to contemporary BR standards but conceptually accorded with the traditional GWR layout for such vehicles.

The Cafeteria Car had an interesting provenance in starting life as one of six kitchen cars (Diagram H31) in fixed 3-vehicle catering sets that formed part of the GWR's articulated trains introduced in 1925. Following the break-up of these units in 1936/7, the kitchen cars were mounted on their own bogies and worked in ordinary mode together with conventional restaurant cars.

However, the preference for kitchens to be combined with either single class or composite dining saloons in a single vehicle meant that a coach containing a kitchen only was an expensive luxury. In 1956, all six were withdrawn and rebuilt with a saloon and bar at either end. In this form they were given the hitherto unused classification of Cafeteria Car (Diagram H49). It was intended that they be employed on special excursion services but it must be doubtful whether they found adequate employment on such duties. All were withdrawn in 1961/2. *Ref PG 1322.*

Above: Because of the unscheduled nature of their activities, departmental workings have little representation in the collections. This is regrettable as these trains could produce unusual combinations of motive power and rolling stock. This was particularly relevant to breakdown trains responding to an accident or emergency as would seem to be the case witnessed here on 15th October 1960. No information is recorded beyond the location described as Langford Bridge, apparently on the Westbury-Salisbury route, to the east of Wylye station.

The train is headed by No 4934 *Hindllip Hall* and banked by large prairie No 5183; both engines give the impression being worked with some urgency. Both cranes are being hauled with match truck and jib leading, and the first is definitely in steam but this cannot be confirmed with the second. In between is inserted a sheeted long wheelbase open wagon of a size and profile suggestive of an Open C or similar. Behind the second crane there is a four-wheel, four compartment passenger coach of which many were built between the early 1880s and 1902 for branch line service. On removal from this work, a number were transferred to departmental duties in the early 1920s. This vehicle appears to have been originally an All First or a First/ Second Composite of mid-1890s vintage. It is coupled next to a standard BR brake van. The use of double locomotives and cranage suggests that a heavy lift is anticipated where the cranes will operate in unison but will be manoeuvred independently of each other. *Ref PG 2459.*

Left: On Sunday, 1st May 1955 "Dukedog" No 9011 was in charge of a permanent way train running wrong line near Swindon under a Class J headcode (mineral or empty wagon train). The front part of the train comprises a Toad, a van and then a Collett-era All Third, apparently for the movement of track personnel. *Ref: PG 545.*

Above: The first Gas Turbine locomotive was ordered by the GWR in January 1946, to be constructed as a joint venture agreed between the company and Metropolitan-Vickers. It commenced mainline testing in early 1952 but was to prove a more troublesome machine than the GWR's second gas turbine which was ordered from Brown-Boveri, Switzerland in late June 1946. The second engine, numbered 18000, first moved in Britain under its own power on 22nd February 1950.

Peter Gray was able to capture the joint venture locomotive, by then numbered 18100, hauling a single Brake Composite up Dainton East on 9th February 1952. This locomotive, accorded the little used classification GT2, could well have been on one of its first long-distance test runs. It entered ordinary service the following April, and in November the South Devon banks were to witness its most memorable performance when it hauled 17 coaches unaided between Plymouth and Newton Abbot. *Ref PG 168.*

Described as in charge of an engineer's special on 26th April 1959, smart 2-6-2T No 6157 was at Swindon with a down working. The train comprises of a Toad, a Macaw, two 5-plank wagons (or equivalent), a crane with jib trailing, another Toad then two more open wagons and finally a BR Brake Van. *RCR Ref: 12901-13999 (321).*

Above: Three generations together at Laira Depot on 30th August 1961. In the foreground stands B-B Class 43 No D853 *Thruster*, built by North British Locomotive Co Ltd. This locomotive officially entered BR service on the day that this photograph was taken; the type was not as successful as the outwardly identical Class 42 and D853 was withdrawn from service on 3rd October 1971. Behind the Warship is Dynamometer Car No DW 150192 which is in the BR version of chocolate and cream. This was a conversion of Hawksworth All Third Diagram C82 No W796W built in August 1946 and rebuilt in 1961. It was also the Dynamometer Car's first outing.

At the rear lurks 0-6-0ST Class 1361 No 1363 (built June 1910) the last shed pilot at Laira Steam and the final, lonely inhabitant of the roundhouse where it stood for some time after official withdrawal in October 1962. On its departure from Plymouth in 1965, it made the short journey to Totnes and start of its life in preservation *RCR Ref R16251-17500 (130).*

Opposite top: One of Dick Riley's panoramas that reminds of the breadth and diversity of interest offered by the railway in the days of steam at stations like Truro. Even the foretaste of what is to come is mitigated by diesel shunter No D3509 working in partnership with a shunter's truck. Great Western steam is on parade in the form of small prairie No 5515 apparently on station pilot duties. Alongside, while carrying Class C fitted parcels head code, No 4083 *Abbotsbury Castle* (again) was shunting wagons despite BR (WR) having inherited a generous supply of tank locomotives for this purpose. No 7812 *Erlestoke Manor* to the right carries a similar head code. The "furniture" adds enormously to the atmosphere – the platelayers trolley in the foreground, the LMS-style brake van in the sidings, the array of wagons in the yard, the Diagram DD4 Cordon at the buffer stops (they always seemed to live at buffer stops when not on the move), the loaded platform trolley waiting for the Manor to clear the board crossing, the platform to the right crowded with parcels and merchandise, and that trademark of any significant Great Western station, the profusion of signals. The date is believed to be April 1960. *RCR Ref 14000-15099 (614).*

Opposite bottom: The GWR was one of the world's largest owners of harbours, yet it was notable how few dock shunters were constructed at Swindon. Based on Class 1392 that had been built by Sharp, Stewart & Co for the Cornwall Minerals Railway and designed by Holcroft in 1910, 0-6-0ST Class 1361 comprised only five locomotives and at least one seems to have been continually allocated to Plymouth Laira for work in the docks and as shed pilot. (Propulsion of loaded wagons up the ramp to the coal stage seemed to be a favourite duty).

On 5th July 1955, No 1364 was down in the docks busy shunting while sandwiched between an outside-framed Siphon G (the number beneath the grime appears to be W1262W) and shunter's truck No W41750, appropriately labelled "Plymouth Docks". The nautical flavour is underlined by the matelot on the extreme right. *RCR Ref 5001-6100 (855).*

Western Region non-passenger trains

Left: 0-6-0PT Class 1366 was introduced in 1934 as an updated version of 0-6-0ST Class 1361 in an evolutionary process that paralleled development of the larger 0-6-0 tank engines. Classes 1361/ 1366 were Swindon's only outside-cylinder 0-6-0 tank engines until the arrival of Class 15xx in 1949. No 1370 was busy shunting wagons on Weymouth Quay on 24th July 1958. A constant traffic hazard was presented by inconsiderately parked vehicles over a short but crowded route shared with cars, lorries, bicycles, pedestrians but where trains took precedent. Railway employees were of necessity adept at the forcible removable of vehicular obstacles. *RCR Ref 11801-12900 (826).*

Bottom: No details are available for this Down train as it approaches the Royal Albert Bridge but the locomotive might be a Modified Hall, followed by an interesting assembly of vehicles that demonstrates how non-passenger bogie vehicles could be inserted into coaching rakes to the inconvenience of those on board. The composition appears to be a combination of two passenger services from different points. The first four vehicles are ex-LMS Period III coaches plus a Passenger Full Brake, followed by an ex-SR utility van, an outside-framed Siphon G, and a Collett All Third immediately before the coach from which the photograph was taken. *RCR Ref 7101-8100 (523).*

Loose ends

To prove that the cover picture of a *Torbay Express*-bedecked freight train was not a one-off event, here is Castle No 5074 *Hampden* on an Up goods at Scotts Bridge between Torre and Kingskerswell on 12th April 1957. This photograph pre-dates the other by a year and shows by the headcode that this service was a Class D Goods train stopping at intermediate stations (15 months later in the cover picture, it was a Class C Goods stopping at intermediate stations). Also, the *Torbay Express*'s train reporting number in 1958 was 142. Changed details such as these illustrate the challenges of train identification, some 60-odd years after the fact. *Ref PG 994.*

Although no goods trains ever formally carried headboards, there was a long tradition of staff giving nicknames to particular services as an aid to their ready identification. For example, the 3.20 am Paddington and return 10.40 am Didcot was known as "Fly"; the 12.35 am Basingstoke and return 1.25 am Oxley (Wolverhampton) was "Cherbourg". By the 1900s, the practice had expanded e.g. the 9.35 pm Paddington and return 1.25 am Oxley had become "Old Man" and the 10.15 pm Paddington to Plymouth (no return) was "Tip".

In 1927 through the pages of *GWR Magazine*, the Chief Goods Manager reminded readers of these practices and initiated a competition for selection of names for vacuum-fitted services (either C-headcode or Accelerated E-headcode services). Although not comprehensive, 75 in these categories were so christened. Traditional nicknames mingled with new inventions to form an eclectic collection.

In some cases, names were based on the principal merchandise shipped e.g. the 8.20 pm Kidderminster-Paddington (*The Carpet*) and the 10.30 pm Reading-Laira (*The Biscuit*).

Destinations were also reflected as with the 10.05 pm Bristol-Leamington (*Spa*), the 7.35 pm Westbury-Manchester (*The Lancashire Lad*) and the 4.58 pm Marazion-Bristol (*The Tre Pol and Pen Flyer*). Others were more esoteric as witness the 4.20 am Westbury-Wolverhampton (*The Moonraker* – the nickname for inhabitants of Wiltshire who were believed to try to rake up the reflection of the moon in a pond in the belief that it was made of cheese) and the 12.30 am Paddington-Bristol (*The Mopper Up* – the last service of the day used to clear out all the remaining vans at Paddington Goods Depot). The 1927 list gained semi-official status but the names were never recorded in the Service Time Tables. In large part, these trains escaped the attention of the enthusiast community by virtue of their timings as 45 of the scheduled departure times were between 7.00 pm and midnight, and 18 started their journeys between 0.01 am and 7.00 am. Only 12 could be expected to complete their journey entirely within daylight hours, depending upon the season.

Perhaps the best known name in fiction was through the Rev Awdry's purloining of *The Flying Skipper* (12.45 am Wolverhampton-Birkenhead) for accident-prone "The Flying Kipper", hauled by Sodor Railway 4-6-0 No 5 *Henry*.

Bibliography

A G Atkins, W Beard, R Tourret	GWR Goods Wagons	OPC 2013
Tony Atkins	GWR Goods Train Working Vol 1	Crécy Publications 2016
Tony Atkins	GWR Goods Train Working Vol 2	Crécy Publications 2017
Tony Atkins	GWR Goods Cartage Vol 2	Crécy Publications 2019
Jeremy Clements	The GWR Exposed	OPC 2015
RA Cooke	Atlas of the GWR as at 1947	Wild Swan Publications 1988
Michael Harris	Great Western Coaches from 1890	David & Charles 1985
Hugh Longworth	British Railways Pre-Nationalisation Coaching Stock Vol 1	OPC 2018
E Lyons	An Historical Survey of Great Western Engine Sheds 1947	OPC 1972
Nigel Pocock & Ian Harrison	Great Western Railway Locomotive Allocations for 1934	Wild Swan Publications
Railway Correspondence & Travel Society	The Locomotives of the Great Western Railway Parts 1-14	1951 et seq
Ian Sixsmith	The 2-8-0T Tank Papers	Irwell Press 2017

An archetypal Down through unfitted freight near Hinksey South Signal Box on a sunny 15th August 1959 with tidily presented Class 2884 2-8-0 No 3808 in charge. By this time the standard BR 16-ton all steel mineral wagon was predominant but ageing pre-war vehicles were still in evidence as with the ex-private owner timber-bodied eight plank wagon behind the tender.

Class 28xx and the later Collett version of 1938 always looked supremely competent on the move with heavy freight trains, an impression that performance on the road did nothing to dispel.
RCR Ref 14000-15099 (122).